GROWING IN
GOD'S
SPIRIT

Jonathan Edwards for Today's Reader

T. M. MOORE, SERIES EDITOR

GROWING IN
GOD'S
SPIRIT

JONATHAN
EDWARDS

EDITED *by* T. M. MOORE

FOREWORD *by* CHARLES COLSON

P U B L I S H I N G
P.O.BOX 817 • PHILLIPSBURG • NEW JERSEY 08865-0817

Page design by Tobias Design
Typesetting by Michelle Feaster

Printed in the United States of America

Library of Congress Cataloging-in-Publication Data

Edwards, Jonathan, 1703–1758.
    Growing in God's spirit / Jonathan Edwards ; edited by
T. M. Moore ; foreword by Charles Colson.
        p.   cm. — (Jonathan Edwards for today's reader)
    Includes bibliographical references.
    ISBN 0-87552-599-7 (pbk.)
    1. Holy Spirit—Early works to 1800. I. Moore, T. M.
(Terry Michael), 1949– II. Title.

BT120.E39 2003
248.4'858—dc21

                                    2003048615

To

James A. R. Johnson

CONTENTS

Series Introduction

Jonathan Edwards (1703–58) is one of the great figures of American church history. Pastor, theologian, evangelist, missionary, husband, and father, Edwards was mightily used of God in his day, and his written works continue to instruct and nurture those who take the time to study them in our own. During his tenure as pastor in the congregational church in Northampton, Massachusetts, Edwards's preaching was the catalyst God's Spirit used to ignite two powerful seasons of revival, including the Great Awakening of the 1740s. He was a man of the Book and a man of the church, devoting himself to the study of God's Word and the work of pastoral care and edification in congregations in New York City, Northampton, and Stockbridge, Massachusetts, where he served as a missionary to native Americans. Although he was elected president of Princeton College in 1757, his untimely death made his tenure there all too brief.

This series is devoted to bringing the sermons and other works of Jonathan Edwards to today's readers in a form that can make for careful reading, thoughtful consideration, lively discussion, and significant growth in the grace and knowledge of the Lord. Edwards preached to farmers and merchants, homemakers and youth, native Americans and small-town professionals. Although his language can seem at times obscure and the logic of his arguments demands our diligent attention, the ordinary people of his day understood him quite well. For nearly three hundred years the works of Jonathan Edwards have instructed and inspired pastors, theologians, and lay readers to a greater love of God and more diligence in spreading God's love to others. This suggests that Edwards's works can serve us in our generation as well.

Edwards's sermons and books are steeped in Scripture and employ careful exposition and rigorous logic to make the glory of the gospel of Jesus Christ clear and compelling. His was indeed a "rational Biblical theology," to borrow a phrase from Dr. John Gerstner, to whom contemporary Christians owe a great debt for his tireless promotion and exposition of the works of the greatest theologian ever to grace the American ecclesiastical scene. For a variety of reasons—among them the demanding nature of Edwards's writing, his use, at times, of archaic or unfamiliar terms, and the difficulty of procuring his works—contemporary readers have not availed themselves of Edwards's sermons and books as much as they might. To their enormous credit, the editors and publishers of the Banner of Truth Trust have labored to overcome these difficulties by making a large number of Edwards's works available in two hefty volumes and by publishing individual sermons and books as separate publications. We are grateful to the Trust for granting us permission to use the edition of Edwards's works prepared by Edward Hickman, first published in 1834 and kept in print by Banner since 1974, for the texts in this series.

The books in this series present the works of Edwards in their original form, as prepared by Hickman, without significant modification in his language. At times we have updated the spelling of a word, altered punctuation, or included Scripture references that Edwards omitted in his texts. We have added headings and subheadings to clarify his arguments, divided some long paragraphs, and portioned each work into short chapters to allow for more careful and considerate reading. We have also incorporated study questions at the end of each chapter to promote thoughtful reflection on the meaning and application of Edwards's arguments and to encourage use of his works in reading and discussion groups.

This series is prepared under the sponsorship of the Jonathan Edwards Institute, whose mission—to promote and nurture a God-entranced worldview—mirrors that of Edwards. We are grateful to Allan Fisher and the staff of P&R Publishing for their vision for and commitment to the plan and purposes of this series. Our hope is that the books in this series will introduce Jonathan Edwards to a new generation of readers and draw them more deeply and passionately into the knowledge of God. We offer them with the hope that God, who sent the Spirit of revival to his church in Edwards's day, might be pleased to use this series as he moves to revive, renew, and restore his glory in his Bride once again.

T. M. Moore
The Jonathan Edwards Institute

❖ ❖ ❖

A series of volumes dedicated to the memory of one of whom many people are unaware needs some explanation. Yet those who have known Jim Johnson understand at once why an exploration of the thought of Jonathan Edwards is a fitting tribute.

Jim was a husband to Martha and father to three sons, Mark, Steve, and David, who are dedicated followers of Christ. He was the mentor and encourager of untold numbers of young men in every walk of life and served as an elder in his church, the Fourth Presbyterian Church in Bethesda, Maryland.

Jim possessed many intellectual qualifications. He was trained in the liberal arts, and he possessed a doctoral degree in jurisprudence. Far from living in academic isolation, he also held various positions within American corporate life, and he worked and moved with ease in government.

He was fully aware of the reality of the fallenness of our humanity. He lived with it and experienced some of its harshest dealings. Yet to each of his callings, and in all his experiences, Jim brought a devotion to Christ and a love of truth. He was an example of one who sought to bring all of life captive to the Word of God.

Jim Johnson serves as a model to those who seek to harness a vital, living relationship with Christ with an honest pursuit of working that out with theological integrity and ethical rigor. When faced with the diagnosis of inoperable cancer, he showed that, as Jonathan Edwards often remarked, Christians can die well. Like Edwards's faith, Jim's was real, true, and practical, and it demanded to be worked out in intellectual, experiential, and ethical ways.

Redeemed by Christ, Jim lived life in gratitude, which is why each one of us who knew him mourned the passing of a great encourager, a powerful mentor, and a humble servant of the Lamb.

Robert M. Norris, senior pastor
Fourth Presbyterian Church
Bethesda, Maryland

FOREWORD

Every Christian is called to press on toward maturity in Christ. True believers, who understand the enormity of Christ's sacrifice and the abundance of the life for which he has redeemed us, hunger and thirst to know him better and love him more. They long to experience his indwelling power, eagerly desire to see the world and everything in it from his perspective, and strive to be equipped to serve him through a wide variety of good works.

In all ages of church history mature believers from every walk of life have made great contributions to the progress of the gospel. They have not always been the giants of the faith we so often think of as we look down the corridors of church history. The saintly Perpetua, dying for her faith in a Roman coliseum, was a young mother whose only crime was her complete inability to denounce the Savior who had died for her. He was too real and too important a part of her life. The headstrong but altogether spiritually serious Francis of Assisi, who literally stripped himself of every earthly possession in order to serve the Lord, showed a maturity of trust that has inspired thousands to follow in his lifestyle of service to others. The humble farm maid who pointed a bony finger in the face of the unconverted Abraham Kuyper and called him to believe in Jesus showed the kind of compassionate boldness that comes only from maturity in the Lord.

I know in my case, once I finally came to understand the truth of the gospel, I was hungry to begin growing in the Lord. I was—and remain today—so grateful for those friends and mentors who steered me into the deep waters of the harbor of Christian truth and showed me how to put down my anchor in the great doctrines of the life of faith. I've grown some since those early days, but I'm daily challenged and excited about the prospect of learning more about Christ and discovering how the life of faith molds and shapes every area of human life and interest.

What a privilege it is to be able to join with a group of friends for this new publication of selected works by Jonathan Edwards, one of the towering figures in modern Christian history. His writings, some of the greatest treasures of the kingdom, have enormously influenced my life and in many ways shaped my theology. This collection will be an invaluable resource for pursuing growth in God's Spirit. I commend your determination to press on toward the upward calling of God in Christ Jesus and pray that you will find this volume of Edwards's sermons particularly helpful in mapping out the vast terrain of spiritual growth that is available to us as disciples of the Lord. May he richly bless and reward your labors as you strive together with others to attain new and more wonderful levels of maturity in Christ.

Charles Colson, founder
Prison Fellowship

INTRODUCTION

I sat delighted as John, a businessman in our church, shared his experience of coming to know the Lord and of growing in him. John runs an international trading company that keeps him very busy—in this country and overseas. He has a lovely family to which he is utterly devoted. Yet he finds time to dedicate, week in and week out, to growing in his Christian faith and encouraging others in the life of discipleship.

I was particularly excited to hear John's story because I had a personal stake in his life, and that in two ways. John had first come to know the Lord more than thirty years ago when Billy Graham conducted a crusade in Knoxville. My father-in-law, Lane Adams, was living in Knoxville at the time, serving as an associate evangelist with Dr. Graham, and had played a large role in helping to bring that ministry to East Tennessee. When I reminded John of that, he quickly commented on the role that Lane had played in his coming to faith and embarking on the process of Christian growth. John had been a member in the same church where Lane and his family worshiped, and his father and Lane were friends.

Now, more than thirty years later, John had called to get together with me just to say thanks for a course I had taught, which had affirmed his calling to disciple other men and honed his skills for more effective service. The infrequency with which such meetings happen in the life of a pastor will make this one forever special to me.

At one point in our time together John looked up from his roast beef sandwich and said, "You know, T. M., I just don't understand it. I look around at the Christians I know, and they don't seem to be all that *excited* about the Lord. It seems like they have time for everything else in life except growing in Christ. I don't want to sound judgmental; I'm just trying to understand why so many Christians appear to be so *nonchalant* about full and abundant life in Christ."

I wish I had an answer. I'm sure every pastor wishes he had an answer. Even Jonathan Edwards must have wished he had an answer for that question. But he did: people, because of their sin and enthrallment with worldly distractions, are ignorant of God's grace and ungrateful for his mercy; they prefer the diversions and entertainments of this world more than the delights of heaven, and this preference, unchecked, will ensure for them an eternity of torment and despair in separation from the Lord.

Respectable ministers today, sensitive to the demands of our seeker-friendly times, would never say such things in public. This fact may well explain why the powerful winds of God's reviving Spirit are yet being held back from his church.

When I think of the works of Jonathan Edwards a string of adjectives comes to mind: urgent, compelling, gracious, profound, uncompromising, rigorously logical, utterly serious. Over the years few theologians have had a more profound effect on my walk with the Lord than the great New England Puritan.

One of the recurrent themes in Edwards's works is the necessity of "pressing on" in the life of faith. He wants us to understand that there is always more of God's grace to experience, more of his truth to learn, more of the beauty of Christ to behold, more power to draw on, more hope to rejoice in, more reasons for giving ourselves without reservation to the Lord Jesus. The Christian life is a journey, a pilgrimage, to heaven, and en route we are called to be scholars in the school of Christ, preparing ourselves in holiness for our eternal dwelling place with God and the Lord Jesus. In one way or another all the sermons, books, and other written works of Edwards underscore and revolve around these themes. The three sermons selected for this book in the series, Jonathan Edwards for Today's Reader, go straight to the heart of this subject. They outline in clear and compelling terms what it means to grow in God's Spirit and how we may begin to do so with greater consistency and delight.

A Divine and Supernatural Light, preached in Edwards's church in Northampton, Massachusetts, probably in 1733, holds forth the promise of making real progress in the life of faith. God, Edwards insisted, is eager to reveal his mysteries to us, to lead us into all truth and show us the deep and wonderful things of his Word. There are powerful and reassuring doctrines to understand; precious promises to lay hold on; profound insights to equip us for daily wisdom; and spiritual delights to contemplate that can fill us with the joy and hope of knowing the Lord Jesus Christ. These great truths—these "divine things" as Edwards called them—can be utterly life-changing, leading us to a greater experience of the goodness of God and to greater faithfulness in his name.

In order to enter more deeply into these great truths we must submit to the teaching of God's Word and seek his Spirit, so that he may unlock these mysteries for us, unfolding them in our minds and emblazoning them on our hearts. We cannot expect to lay hold on these truths by the mere exercise of human reason or understanding. Rather, we must look to God, through faith in Jesus Christ, and learn what it means to seek and trust him as he reveals himself to us in his Word. This is the way to holiness, and holiness, as Edwards will explain in the third sermon of this series, is the proper calling and pastime of the believer.

Imagine the implications of such a claim: the God who made heaven and earth, who sustains the universe and all things in it by the power of his Word; the God who sent his Son to accomplish the salvation of sinners, has more truth, more beauty, more glory, more spiritual insight to communicate to all who will look to him in faith. When they do look to him, they find his Word amazing, marvelous, exciting, and life-changing. For the light of truth that God has prepared for us holds hope, power, joy, and purpose for all who put their trust in Jesus Christ. God is eager and able to give this light to us, but we must come frequently and faithfully to him.

This is the theme of our second message, *Christian Knowledge*. If the thrust of *A Divine and Supernatural Light* is to encourage us to see how willing and able God is to lead us more deeply into the life of Christian growth, *Christian Knowledge* intends to outline our responsibility in pursuing such a life. As Paul told the Philippians, God is at work within us to give us the will to follow him and to carry out his good pleasure in our lives; we, however, must work hard if we are to see the promise of the life of faith come to fruition (Phil. 2:12–13).

This is what Edwards is getting at in this second message. There is a knowledge of divine things available to us. God, as we have seen, is more than willing to impart divine light to our minds and hearts. Yet we must reach out for it, lay hold on it, and make it part of our lives. We should be as dutiful about seeking divine light as we are about our daily business. It's hard work, and it takes time. But growing in God's Spirit is our calling as disciples—a word, Edwards points out, that means "learners." If our Lord calls us "learners," surely he intends that no small part of our time and energy should be devoted to this task. If our approach to growing in the knowledge of divine things is merely "by the bye"—nonchalant—we cannot expect to know the full riches of our salvation, and we may well be showing that we have no true heart of gratitude or love for God.

All right, but how do we *do* this? How do we grow in Christian knowledge? Edwards obliges with seven concise and helpful recommendations that we will use as the basis for developing our personal plans for growing in God's Spirit.

The third sermon, *The Christian Pilgrim,* preached in September 1733, sets the life of faith into its proper eternal context. Edwards shows us that, as the old gospel song declares, "This world is not my home / I'm just a-passin' through." We were made for heaven. Life on this earth is merely preparation for eternity. Here, as we grow in divine light and Christian knowledge, we increase in holiness, gaining every day more and more a foretaste of that eternal feast of joy and glory that awaits us in the heavenly realm. Such a view of the life of faith can help us to deal properly with death—that of loved ones in the Lord, as well as our own. We need to see our whole life as a journey toward heaven and not carry around too much baggage from this world as we make our way to the next. That way we'll be able to keep our eyes on our destination and devote ourselves daily to the task of preparing to live with the Lord forever.

In these three sermons Edwards holds out for us a vision of the life of faith that is infused with a transcendent perspective, delights in the prospect of heaven and the presence of God, and takes seriously the challenge and privilege of growing in God's Spirit. Today, when so many Christians embrace a need-centered approach to following Christ, I can think of few more needful messages. We are so busy fixating on our needs in this world that we have lost sight of the glories of heaven—where we will spend eternity! Our vision of the life of faith revolves around feeling better about ourselves or learning to cope with the struggles of being human at the beginning of the twenty-first century. We spend very little time thinking about the beauty of the Lord, anchoring in the deep waters of biblical truth, or longing for heaven and a home where there are no more sorrows and no more tears. Edwards's messages provide a much-needed corrective to our vision of the Christian life and our sense of what God has called us to as his people here and now.

You may want to read each message through in its entirety before going back to study the message section by section. That way you'll get an overview of Edwards's sense of what it means to grow in God's Spirit, and you'll be prepared to plunge more deeply into his thoughts as you work chapter by chapter through the pages that follow. You might gain the most benefit from this book by studying with a friend or a group of friends. As Edwards observed, it is important to "improve conversation" about spiritual matters, which can be done only in the company of others. Take your time, answer each of the study questions, and let Edwards reach to your heart and mind the way he did to his congregation nearly three hundred years ago. God's Word, ministered through the works of Jonathan Edwards, can lead you to a life-changing experience of growing in God's Spirit.

I want to thank John Bishop for his generous and faithful work in helping to get this first book in the series ready. My prayer—and that of the Jonathan Edwards Institute, who conceived this project in the first place—is that readers will find studying the works of Jonathan Edwards a means to entering more fully into the divine light of God's truth and to growing in his Spirit.

❈ *Part 1* ❈

A DIVINE AND
SUPERNATURAL LIGHT

❊ Chapter 1 ❊

GOD ALONE GIVES
SPIRITUAL KNOWLEDGE

In this brief introduction to this first message, Edwards shows that spiritual knowledge, that is, the knowledge of divine truth, is imparted by God alone. While we may learn many things from others about life in general, only God can reveal the secrets of revelation to men and women. They are thus "blessed" of God who have received such illumination of divine truth by the Spirit of God.

MATTHEW 16:17
And Jesus answered and said unto him, Blessed art thou, Simon Bar-Jona: for flesh and blood hath not revealed it unto thee, but my Father, which is in heaven.

Christ addresses these words to Peter upon occasion of his professing his faith in him as the Son of God. Our Lord was inquiring of his disciples who men said that he was; not that he needed to be informed, but only to introduce and give occasion to what follows. They answer that some said he was John the Baptist, and some Elijah, and others Jeremiah, or one of the prophets. When they had thus given an account who others said that he was, Christ asks them who they said that he was? Simon Peter, whom we find always zealous and forward, was the first to answer: he readily replied to the question, *Thou art Christ, the Son of the living God.*

THE BLESSING OF PETER

Upon this occasion, Christ says as he does *to* him and *of* him in the text: in which we may observe,

That he knew Jesus to be the Christ

1. That Peter is pronounced blessed on this account— *Blessed art thou*—"Thou art a happy man that thou art not ignorant of this, that I am *Christ, the Son of the living God.* Thou art distinguishingly happy. Others are blinded, and have dark and deluded apprehensions, as you have given an account, some thinking that I am Elijah, and some that I am Jeremiah, and some one thing, and some another; but none of them are thinking right, all of them misled. Happy art thou that art so distinguished as to know the truth in this matter."

That God had revealed this to him

2. The evidence of this his happiness declared; viz.,[1] that God, and he *only*, had *revealed it* to him. This is an evidence of his being *blessed.*

1. Namely.

First, as it shows how peculiarly favored he was of God above others: q.d.[2] "How highly favored art thou that others, wise and great men, the scribes, Pharisees, and Rulers, and the nation in general, are left in darkness to follow their own misguided apprehensions; and that thou shouldst be singled out, as it were, by name, that my heavenly Father should thus set his love on *thee, Simon Bar-Jonah.* This argues thee *blessed,* that thou shouldst thus be the object of God's distinguishing love."

Second, it evidences his blessedness also, as it intimates that this knowledge is above any that *flesh* and *blood* can *reveal.* "This is such knowledge as only my *Father which is in heaven* can give: it is too high and excellent to be communicated by such means as other knowledge is. Thou art *blessed* that thou knowest what God alone can teach thee."

GOD THE AUTHOR
OF ALL KNOWLEDGE

The original[3] of this knowledge is here declared, both negatively and positively. *Positively,* as God is here declared the author of it. *Negatively,* as it is declared that *flesh and blood* had *not revealed it.*

All moral knowledge and business skill from God

God is the author of all knowledge and understanding whatsoever. He is the author of all moral prudence and of

2. As if he said.
3. The origin or source.

the skill that men have in their secular business. Thus it is said of all in Israel that were *wise-hearted*, and skilled in embroidering, that God had *filled* them *with the spirit of wisdom* (Exod. 28:3).

Yet flesh and blood reveals it

God is the author of such knowledge; yet so that *flesh and blood reveals it*. Mortal men are capable of imparting the knowledge of human arts and sciences, and skill in temporal affairs. God is the author of such knowledge by those means: *flesh and blood* is employed as the *mediate* or *second* cause of it: he conveys it by the power and influence of natural means.

God alone the author of spiritual knowledge

But this spiritual knowledge spoken of in the text is what God is the author of, and none else: he *reveals it,* and *flesh and blood reveals it not.* He imparts this knowledge immediately, not making use of any intermediate natural causes, as he does in other knowledge.

PROPOSITION AND PREVIEW

What had passed in the preceding discourse naturally occasioned Christ to observe this; because the disciples had been telling how others did not know him, but were generally mistaken about him, divided and confounded in their opinions of him: but Peter had declared his assured faith that he was the *Son of God.* Now it was natural to observe how it was not *flesh and blood* that had *revealed it to him,* but God; for if this knowledge were dependent on natural causes or means, how came it to pass that they, a company of poor fishermen, illiterate men and persons of low education, attained to the knowledge of the truth; while the scribes and Pharisees, men of vastly higher advantages and greater knowledge and sagacity in other matters, remained ignorant? This could be owing only to the gracious and distinguishing influence and revelation of the Spirit of God.

Hence, what I would make the subject of my present discourse from these words is this doctrine: That there is such a thing as a spiritual and divine light, immediately imparted to the soul by God, of a different nature from any that is obtained by natural means. And on this subject I would,

   I. Show what this divine light is,
  II. How it is given immediately by God, and not obtained by natural means.
 III. Show the truth of the doctrine.

And then conclude with a brief improvement.[4]

STUDY QUESTIONS

1. How is Edwards using the term *blessed* in this message? Read Psalm 1. How does the psalmist contrast the life of

4. Application.

those who are "blessed" (Hebrew *ashre,* "completely happy and fulfilled") with that of those who are not? What seems to be the key to being thus blessed?

2. Edwards insists that all knowledge comes from God. He cites moral prudence, skill in business, and wisdom in everyday living as examples of such knowledge. How do people come by such knowledge today? According to Edwards, how is God involved in this process of learning? How should people respond to all the various kinds of knowledge they receive and make use of each day? Do people generally do this? Why or why not?

3. According to Edwards, knowledge of spiritual truth comes *immediately* by God's Spirit. This agrees with what Paul says in 2 Corinthians 3:12–18. What do Edwards's claim and this passage suggest about the potential of what might happen, say, when you are having your daily devotions, listening to a sermon, or studying a message like this one? Is God constrained by our level of education in revealing such things to us? How might a person better prepare himself to hear whatever God's Spirit might want to make known to him?

4. Can you think of a time when you came to understand some spiritual truth that had been previously unknown to you or difficult to comprehend? Describe the experience. Can you see that it was only because the Spirit of God at last made this clear to you that you were able to grasp it? Keeping in mind Edwards's remarks concerning what this work of illumination suggests about God's love for us,

how should such special attention on the part of God's Spirit affect our hearts toward God?

5. In this first part of our study, Edwards is going to teach us about the nature of divine illumination and how we come to receive it. How do you hope to benefit from the study of the three sermons in this book, *Growing in God's Spirit*? What would you like to see different in your attitude toward God and his Word? Your practice of spiritual disciplines? Your daily walk with the Lord? Set two or three personal goals for your study of the three messages in this volume. Write them out below.

❧ Chapter 2 ❧

THE NATURE OF
DIVINE LIGHT

Before proceeding to define more carefully the nature of divine light, Edwards clears up certain misunderstandings about where such light may be found or in what it consists. He shows that unregenerate people are capable of certain "spiritual" experiences; however, these have more to do with the natural inclinations of such things as conscience than with the illuminating work of the Spirit. Conviction of sin, strong impressions on the imagination, "new revelations," and common religious sensibilities are not the divine light of which Edwards speaks. Having shown what divine and supernatural light is not, Edwards proceeds to define it more clearly and to show how it is given. This light is not merely understood with the mind but experienced with the heart, leading to a sense of God's beauty and glory, to delighting in him and his truth, and to finding pleasure in the things of the Lord. Such a knowledge of divine light comes through the Word of God by the work of the Holy Spirit.

I. I would show what this spiritual and divine light is. And in order to it, would show,

First, in a few things what it is not. And here,

What Divine Light Is Not

Not mere conviction of sin and misery

1. Those convictions that natural men may have of their sin and misery are not this spiritual and divine light. Men in a natural condition may have convictions of the guilt that lies upon them, and of the anger of God, and their danger of divine vengeance. Such convictions are from the light of truth. That some sinners have a greater conviction of their guilt and misery than others is because some have more light, or more of an apprehension of truth, than others. And this light and conviction may be from the Spirit of God; the Spirit convinces men of sin; but yet nature is much more concerned in it than in the communication of that spiritual and divine light that is spoken of in the doctrine; it is from the Spirit of God only as assisting natural principles, and not as infusing any new principles.

Common grace differs from special, in that it influences only by assisting of nature; and not by imparting grace, or bestowing anything above nature. The light that is obtained is wholly natural, or of no superior kind to what mere nature attains to, though more of that kind be obtained than would be obtained if men were left wholly to themselves; or, in other words, common grace only assists the faculties of the soul to do that more fully which they do by nature, as natural conscience or reason will by mere nature make a man sensible of guilt, and will accuse and condemn him when he has done amiss. Conscience is a principle natural to men; and the work it doth naturally, or of itself, is to give an apprehension of right and wrong, and to suggest to the mind the relation that there is between right and wrong and a retribution.

The Spirit of God, in those convictions which unregenerate men sometimes have, assists conscience to do this work in a further degree than it would do if they were left to themselves. He helps it against those things that tend to stupefy it, and obstruct its exercise. But in the renewing and sanctifying work of the Holy Ghost, those things are wrought in the soul that are above nature, and of which there is nothing of the like kind in the soul by nature; and they are caused to exist in the soul habitually, and according to such a stated constitution or law that lays such a foundation for exercises in a continued course as is called a principle of nature. Not only are remaining principles assisted to do their work more freely and fully, but those principles are restored that were utterly destroyed by the fall; and the mind thenceforward habitually exerts those acts that the dominion of sin had made it as wholly destitute of as a dead body is of vital acts.

The Spirit of God acts in a very different manner in the one case from what he doth in the other. He may indeed act upon the mind of a natural man, but he acts in the mind of a saint as an indwelling vital principle. He acts upon the mind of an unregenerate person as an extrinsic occasional agent; for in acting upon them, he doth not unite himself to them; for notwithstanding all his influence that they may possess, they are still sensual, having not the Spirit (Jude 19). But he unites himself with the mind of a saint, takes him for his temple, actuates and influences him as a new supernatural principle of life and action. There is this difference, that the Spirit of God, in acting in the soul of a godly man, exerts and communicates himself there in his own proper nature.

Holiness is the proper nature of the Spirit of God.[1] The Holy Spirit operates in the minds of the godly by uniting himself to them and living in them, exerting his own nature in the exercise of their faculties. The Spirit of God may act upon a creature, and yet not, in acting, communicate himself. The Spirit of God may act upon inanimate creatures; as, *the Spirit moved upon the face of the waters,* in the beginning of creation; so the Spirit of God may act upon the minds of men many ways, and communicate himself no more than when he acts upon an inanimate creature. For instance, he may excite thoughts in them, may assist their natural reason and understanding, or may assist other natural principles, and this without any union with the soul, but may act, as it were, upon an external object. But as he acts in his holy influences and spiritual operations, he acts in a way of peculiar communication of himself; so that the subject is thence denominated spiritual.

Not mere impressions on the imagination

2. This spiritual and divine light does not consist in any impression made upon the imagination. It is no mere

1. Mark this mention of holiness. It will return in each sermon in our series.

impression upon the mind, as though one saw anything with the bodily eyes. It is no imagination or idea of an outward light or glory, or any beauty of form or countenance, or a visible luster or brightness of any object. The imagination may be strongly impressed with such things; but this is not spiritual light. Indeed when the mind has a lively discovery of spiritual things and is greatly affected by the power of divine light, it may, and probably very commonly doth, much affect the imagination; so that impressions of an outward beauty or brightness may *accompany* those spiritual discoveries. But spiritual light is not that impression upon the imagination, but an exceedingly different thing. Natural men may have lively impressions on their imaginations; and we cannot determine but that the devil, who transforms himself into an angel of light, may cause imaginations of an outward beauty, or visible glory, and of sounds and speeches, and other such things; but these are things of a vastly inferior nature to spiritual light.

Not "new revelations" apart from Scripture

3. This spiritual light is not the suggesting of any new truths or propositions not contained in the Word of God. This suggesting of new truths or doctrines to the mind, independent of any antecedent revelation of those propositions, either in word or writing, is inspiration; such as the prophets and apostles had, and such as some enthusiasts pretend to. But this spiritual light that I am speaking of is quite a different thing from inspiration. It reveals no new doctrine, it suggests no new proposition to the mind, it

teaches no new thing of God, or Christ, or another world, not taught in the Bible, but only gives a due apprehension of those things that are taught in the Word of God.

Not mere religious insight or affection

4. It is not every affecting view that men have of religious things that is this spiritual and divine light. Men by mere principles of nature are capable of being affected with things that have a special relation to religion as well as other things. A person by mere nature, for instance, may be liable to be affected with the story of Jesus Christ, and the sufferings he underwent, as well as by any other tragical story. He may be the more affected with it from the interest he conceives mankind to have in it. Yea, he may be affected with it without believing it; as well as a man may be affected with what he reads in a romance, or sees acted in a stage play. He may be affected with a lively and eloquent description of many pleasant things that attend the state of the blessed in heaven, as well as his imagination entertained by a romantic description of the pleasantness of fairy land, or the like. And a common belief of the truth of such things, from education or otherwise, may help forward their affection.

We read in Scripture of many that were greatly affected with things of a religious nature, who yet are there represented as wholly graceless, and many of them very ill men. A person therefore may have affecting views of the things of religion and yet be very destitute of spiritual light. Flesh and blood may be the author of this: one man may give another an affective view of divine things with but common assistance; but God alone can give a spiritual discovery of them.

But I proceed to show,

WHAT DIVINE LIGHT IS

Second, positively what this spiritual and divine light is.

Divine light defined

And it may be thus described: a true sense of the divine excellency of the things revealed in the Word of God, and conviction of the truth and reality of them thence arising. This spiritual light primarily consists in the former of these, viz., a real sense and apprehension of the divine excellency of things revealed in the Word of God. A spiritual and saving conviction of the truth and reality of these things arises from such a sight of their divine excellency and glory; so that this conviction of their truth is an effect and natural consequence of this sight of their divine glory. There is therefore in this spiritual light,

A sense of the divinity and excellency of the things of faith

I. A true sense of the divine and superlative excellency of the things of religion; a real sense of the excellency of God and Jesus Christ, and of the work of redemption, and the ways and works of God revealed in the gospel. There is a divine and superlative glory in these things; and excellency that is of a vastly higher kind, and more sublime nature, than in other things; a glory greatly distinguishing them from all that is earthly and temporal. He that is spiritually enlightened truly apprehends and sees it, or has a sense of it. He does not merely rationally believe that God is glorious, but he has a sense of the gloriousness of God in his heart. There is not only a rational belief that God is holy, and that holiness is a good thing, but there is a sense of the loveliness of God's holiness. There is not only a speculative judging that God is gracious, but a sense how amiable God is on account of the beauty of this divine attribute.

There is a twofold knowledge of good of which God has made the mind of man capable. The first, that which is merely notional; as when a person only speculatively judges that anything is, by the agreement of mankind, good or excellent, viz., that which is most to general advantage, and between which and a reward there is a suitableness—and the like. And the other is that which consists in the sense of the heart; as when the heart is sensible of pleasure and delight in the presence of the idea of it. In the former is exercised merely the speculative faculty, or the understanding, in distinction from the will or disposition of the soul. In the latter, the will, or inclination, of the heart are mainly concerned.

Thus there is a difference between having an *opinion* that God is holy and gracious, and having a *sense* of the loveliness and beauty of that holiness and grace. There is a difference between having a rational judgment that honey is sweet, and having a sense of its sweetness. A man may have the former that knows not how honey tastes; but a man cannot have the latter unless he has an idea of the taste of honey in his mind. So there is a difference between believing that a person is beautiful, and having a sense of his beauty. The former may be obtained by hearsay, but the latter only by seeing the countenance. When the heart is sensible of the beauty and amiableness of a thing, it necessarily feels pleasure in the apprehension. It is implied in a person's being heartily sensible of the loveliness of a thing, that the idea of it is pleasant to his soul; which is a far different thing from having a rational opinion that it is excellent.

A conviction of the truth of divine things

2. There arises from this sense of the divine excellency of things contained in the Word of God, a conviction of the truth and reality of them; and that either indirectly or directly.

First, indirectly, and that two ways.

(1) As the prejudices of the heart, against the truth of divine things, are hereby removed; so that the mind becomes susceptive to the due force of rational arguments for their truth. The mind of a man is naturally full of prejudices against divine truth. It is full of enmity against the doctrines of the gospel; which is a disadvantage to those arguments that prove their truth, and causes them to lose their force upon the mind. But when a person has discovered[2] to him the divine excellency of Christian doctrines, this destroys the enmity, removes those prejudices, sancti-

2. Disclosed.

fies the reason, and causes it to lie open to the force of arguments for their truth.

Hence was the different effect that Christ's miracles had to convince the disciples, from what they had to convince the scribes and Pharisees. Not that they had a stronger reason, or had their reason more improved; but their reason was sanctified, and those blinding prejudices that the scribes and Pharisees were under were removed by the sense of the excellency of Christ and his doctrine.

(2) It not only removes the hindrances of reason, but positively helps reason. It makes even the speculative notions more lively. It engages the attention of the mind, with more fixedness and intenseness to that kind of objects; which causes it to have a clearer view of them, and enables it more clearly to see their mutual relations, and occasions to take more notice of them. The ideas themselves that otherwise are dim and obscure, are by this means impressed with greater strength and have a light cast upon them; so that the mind can better judge of them. As he that beholds objects on the face of the earth, when the light of the sun is cast upon them, is under greater advantage to discern them in their true forms and natural relations than he that sees them in a dim twilight. The mind being sensible of the excellency of divine objects, dwells upon them with delight; and the powers of the soul are more awakened and enlivened to employ themselves in the contemplation of them, and exert themselves more fully and much more to purpose. The beauty of the objects draws on the faculties, and draws forth their exercises; so that reason itself is under

far greater advantage for its proper and free exercises, and to attain its proper end, free of darkness and delusion. But,

Second, a true sense of the divine excellency of the things of God's Word doth more directly and immediately convince us of their truth; and that because the excellency of these things is so superlative. There is a beauty in them so divine and God-like, that it greatly and evidently distinguishes them from things merely human, or that of which men are the inventors and authors; a glory so high and great, that when clearly seen, commands assent to their divine reality. When there is an actual and lively discovery of this beauty and excellency, it will not allow of any such thought as that it is the fruit of men's invention. This is a kind of intuitive and immediate evidence, because they see a divine, and transcendent, and most evidently distinguishing glory in them; such a glory as, if clearly seen, does not leave room to doubt of their being of God, and not of men.

Such a conviction of the truths of religion as this, arising from a sense of their divine excellency, is included in saving faith. And this original of it is that by which it is most essentially distinguished from that common assent of which unregenerate men are capable.

How Divine Light Is Given by God

II. I now proceed to the *second* thing proposed, viz., to show how this light is immediately given by God, and not obtained by natural means. And here,

Natural faculties are involved

1. It is not intended that the natural faculties[3] are not used in it. They are the subject of this light; and in such a manner that they are not merely passive, but active in it. God, in letting this light into the soul, deals with man according to his nature, and makes use of his rational faculties. But yet this light is not the less immediately from God for that; the faculties are made use of as the subject, and not as the cause. As the use we make of our eyes in beholding various objects, when the sun arises, is not the cause of the light that discovers those objects to us.

Outward means also involved

2. It is not intended that outward means have no concern in this affair. It is not in this affair, as in inspiration, where new truths are suggested; for by this light is given only a due apprehension of the same truths that are revealed in the Word of God; and therefore it is not given without the Word. The gospel is employed in this affair. The light is "the light of the glorious gospel of Christ" (2 Cor. 4:4). The gospel is as a glass, by which this light is conveyed to us (1 Cor. 13:12): "now we see through a glass." But,

Only God's Spirit gives divine light

3. When it is said that this light is given immediately by God, and not obtained by natural means,

3. He means such things as reading and understanding, thinking and reasoning.

hereby is intended that it is given by God without making use of any means that operate by their own power of natural force. God makes use of means; but it is not as mediate causes to produce this effect. There are not truly any second causes of it; but it is produced by God immediately. The Word of God is no proper cause of this effect; but is made use of only to convey to the mind the subject matter of this saving instruction: and this indeed it doth convey to us by natural force or influence. It conveys to our minds these doctrines; it is the cause of a notion of them in our heads, but not of the sense of their divine excellency in our hearts. Indeed a person cannot have spiritual light without the Word. But that does not argue, that the Word properly causes that light. The mind cannot see the excellency of any doctrine, unless that doctrine be first in the mind; but seeing the excellency of the doctrine may be immediately from the Spirit of God; though the conveying of the doctrine or proposition itself may be by the Word. So that the notions which are the subject matter of this light are conveyed to the mind by the Word of God; but that the due sense of the heart, wherein this light formally consists, is immediately from the Spirit of God. As for instance, the notion that there is a Christ, and that Christ is holy and gracious, is conveyed to the mind by the Word of God; but the sense of the excellency of Christ by reason of that holiness and grace is nevertheless immediately the work of the Holy Spirit.

STUDY QUESTIONS

1. Reread this section, paying careful attention to each time Edwards contrasts the conveying of spiritual truth to the mind with the sensing of spiritual truth in the heart. What is the difference between these? What is the role of each in discovering divine light? Which is the genuine experience of divine light, and why? Would you say that this is typically the way you apprehend spiritual truth? Why or why not?

2. According to Edwards, how can we know when we have truly come to experience divine light? What is the role of such things as "sensing" (or, experiencing and being convinced), delighting in, knowing pleasure, and so forth in receiving divine light? To what extent do such things as these characterize your relationship with God and his truth?

3. Edwards insists that the Word of God is the source of divine light. However, he makes a distinction between the Scriptures as an object and source of revelation and the work of the Spirit in making that revelation known to us. Why is each—the Word and the Spirit—important in the process of entering into divine and supernatural light—of growing in God's Spirit? Can we expect to grow in God's Spirit without one or the other of these? Why not?

4. Edwards guards against thinking that this divine light might be nothing more than a merely subjective experience—something we might "see" or envision, or some new idea about God we might "discover." How does he make

this point against mere subjectivity? What, according to Edwards, may well be the source of such subjective insights? What does Edwards consider to be the role of the Bible in the work of God's Spirit as He leads us into divine light? How do the faculties of thinking and reasoning work in this process?

5. Edwards cautions against thinking that strong feelings, prompted by many different kinds of stimuli, are evidence of having entered into divine light. Do you see evidence that Christians today may be thinking that strong emotions—in worship, for example—are a valid indication of being in communication with God's Spirit? Do you think Edwards would agree? Why or why not? How might he advise such people on this matter? How does Edwards distinguish between the work of the Spirit upon a person and his work within him or her?

❧ Chapter 3 ❧

THE PROOF AND BENEFITS OF DIVINE LIGHT

Edwards now moves to prove his doctrine of divine and supernatural light by recourse to Scripture and reason and to indicate the excellencies and benefits of the knowledge of God. He concludes with some exhortations to seek this knowledge above all else—the means to which he will explain more fully in the next sermon—and to point out what we might hope to realize from devoting ourselves to this effort.

I come now,

III. To show the truth of the doctrine; that is, to show that there is such a thing as that spiritual light that has been described, thus immediately let into the mind by God. And here I would show briefly, that this doctrine is both *scriptural* and *rational*.

THE SCRIPTURAL PROOF OF THIS DOCTRINE

Saints possess this knowledge and sight of God

First, it is scriptural. My text is not only full to the purpose, but it is a doctrine with which the Scripture abounds.

We are there abundantly taught that the saints differ from the ungodly in this, that they have the knowledge of God, and a sight of God, and of Jesus Christ. I shall mention but a few texts out of many: "Whosoever sinneth, hath not seen him, nor known him" (1 John 3:6). "He that doth good, is of God: but he that doth evil, hath not seen God" (3 John 11). "The world seeth me no more; but ye see me" (John 14:19). "And this is eternal life, that they might know thee, the only true God, and Jesus Christ whom thou hast sent" (John 17:3). This knowledge, or sight of God and Christ, cannot be a mere speculative knowledge; because it is spoken of as that wherein they differ from the ungodly. And by these Scriptures it must not only be a different knowledge in degree and circumstances, and different in its effects; but it must be entirely different in nature and kind.

This knowledge and sight of God given immediately by God

And this light and knowledge is always spoken of as immediately given of God; "At that time Jesus answered and said, I thank thee, O Father, Lord of heaven and earth, because thou hast hid these things from the wise and prudent, and hast revealed them unto babes. Even so, Father: for so it seemed good in thy sight. All things are delivered unto me of my Father: and no man knoweth . . . the Father, save the Son, and he to whomsoever the Son will reveal him" (Matt. 11:25–27). Here this effect is ascribed exclusively to the arbitrary operation and gift of God bestowing knowledge on whom he will, and distinguishing those with it who have the least natural advantage or means for knowledge, even babes, when it is denied to the wise and prudent. And imparting this knowledge is here appropriated to the Son of God, as his sole prerogative.

And again, "For God who commanded the light to shine out of darkness, hath shined in our hearts, to give the light of the knowledge of the glory of God, in the face of Jesus Christ" (2 Cor. 4:6). This plainly shows that there is a discovery of the divine superlative glory and excellency of God and Christ, peculiar to the saints; and also, that it is immediately from God, as light from the sun: and that it is the immediate effect of his power and will. For it is compared to God's creating the light by his powerful word in the beginning of the creation; and is said to be by the Spirit of the Lord, in the eighteenth verse of the preceding chapter.[1] God is spoken of as giving the knowledge of Christ in conversion, as of what before was hidden and unseen: "But when it pleased God, who separated me from my mother's womb, and called my by his grace, to reveal his Son in me" (Gal. 1:15–16).

The Scripture also speaks plainly of such a knowledge of the Word of God, as has been described, as the immediate gift of God: "Open thou mine eyes, that I may behold wondrous things out of thy law" (Ps. 119:18). What could the psalmist mean, when he begged God to open his eyes? Was he ever blind? Might he not have resort to the law and see every word and sentence in it when he pleased? And what could he mean by those wondrous things? Were they the wonderful stories of the creation, the deluge, and Is-

1. 2 Cor. 3:18.

rael's passing through the Red Sea, and the like? Were not his eyes open to read these strange things when he would? Doubtless by wondrous things in God's law, he had respect to those distinguishing and wonderful excellencies, and marvelous manifestations of the divine perfections and glory, contained in the commands and doctrines of the Word, and those works and counsels of God that were there revealed. So the Scripture speaks of a knowledge of God's dispensation and covenant of mercy and way of grace toward his people, as peculiar to the saints, and given only by God: "The secret of the Lord is with them that fear him; and he will show them his covenant" (Ps. 25:14).

What arises from this divine light

And that a true and saving belief of the truth of religion is that which arises from such a discovery, is also what the Scripture teaches, as in John 6:40: "And this is the will of him that sent me, that every one that seeth the Son, and believeth on him, may have everlasting life"; where it is plain that a true faith is what arises from a spiritual sight of Christ. And in John 17:6–8: "I have manifested thy name unto the men which thou gavest me out of the world. . . . Now they have known that all things whatsoever thou hast given me, are of thee. For I have given unto them the words which thou gavest me, and they have received them, and have known surely that I came out from thee, and they have believed that thou didst send me"; where Christ's manifesting God's name to the disciples, or giving them the knowledge of God, was that whereby they knew that

Christ's doctrine was of God, and that Christ himself proceeded from him, and was sent by him. Again, in John 12:44–46: "Jesus cried and said, He that believeth on me, believeth not on me, but on him that sent me. And he that seeth me, seeth him that sent me. I am come a light into the world, that whosoever believeth on me, should not abide in darkness." There believing in Christ, and spiritually seeing him, are parallel.

Those without such light condemned

Christ condemns the Jews, that they did not know that he was the Messiah, and that his doctrine was true, from an inward and distinguishing taste and relish of what was divine, in Luke 12:56–57. He having there blamed the Jews, that though they could discern the face of the sky and of the earth, and signs of the weather, they could not discern those times—or as it is expressed in Matthew, the signs of those times—adds, "yea, and why even of your own selves, judge ye not what is right?" i.e., without extrinsic signs. Why have ye not that sense of true excellency, whereby ye may distinguish that which is holy and divine? Why have ye not that savor of the things of God, by which you may see the distinguishing glory, and evident divinity, of me and my doctrine?

Those possessing divine light assured

The apostle Peter mentions it as what gave him and his companions good and well-grounded assurance of the truth of the gospel, that they had seen the divine glory of Christ. "For we have not followed cunningly devised fables, when we made known unto you the power and coming of our Lord Jesus Christ, but were eyewitnesses of his majesty" (2 Peter 1:16). The apostle has respect to that visible glory of Christ which they saw in his transfiguration: that glory was so divine, having such an ineffable appearance and semblance of divine holiness, majesty, and grace, that it evidently denoted him to be a divine person. But if a sight of Christ's outward glory might give a rational assurance of his divinity, why may not an apprehension of his spiritual glory do so too? Doubtless Christ's spiritual glory is in itself as distinguishing, and as plainly shows his divinity, as his outward glory, nay, a great deal more: for his spiritual glory is that wherein his divinity consists: and the outward glory of his transfiguration showed him to be divine, only as it was a remarkable image or representation of that spiritual glory. Doubtless, therefore, he may say, I have not followed cunningly devised fables, but have been an eyewitness of his majesty, upon as good grounds as the apostle, when he had respect to the outward glory of Christ that he had seen. But this brings me to what was proposed next, viz., to show that,

The Rational Proof of This Doctrine

Second, this doctrine is rational.

That divine things should be more excellent

1. It is rational to suppose that there is really such an excellency in divine things—so transcendent and exceedingly different from what is in other things—that, if it were

seen, would most evidently distinguish them. We cannot rationally doubt but that things divine, which appertain to the Supreme Being, are vastly different from things that are human; that there is a high, glorious, and God-like excellency in them that does most remarkably difference them from the things that are seen of men; insomuch that if the difference were but seen, it would have a convincing, satisfying influence upon anyone, that they are divine. What reason can be offered against it? Unless we would argue, that God is not remarkably distinguished in glory from men.

If Christ should now appear to anyone as he did on the mount at his transfiguration; or if he should appear to the world in his heavenly glory, as he will do at the day of judgment; without doubt, his glory and majesty would be such as would satisfy everyone that he was a divine person, and that religion was true: and it would be a most reasonable and well-grounded conviction too. And why may there not be that stamp of divinity, or divine glory, on the Word of God, on the scheme and doctrine of the gospel, that may be in like manner distinguishing and as rationally convincing, provided it be but seen? It is rational to suppose, that when God speaks to the world, there should be something in his Word vastly different from men's word. Supposing that God never had spoken to the world, but we had notice that he was about to reveal himself from heaven, and speak to us immediately himself, of that he should give us a book of his own inditing;[2] after what manner should we expect that he would speak? Would it not be rational to suppose

2. Authorship.

that his speech would be exceeding different from men's speech, that there should be such an excellency and sublimity in his Word, such a stamp of wisdom, holiness, majesty, and other divine perfections, that the word of men, yea of the wisest men, should appear mean and base in comparison of it? Doubtless it would be thought rational to expect this, and unreasonable to think otherwise.

When a wise man speaks in the exercise of his wisdom, there is something in everything he says that is very distinguishable from the talk of a little child. So, without doubt, and much more, is the speech of God to be distinguished from that of the wisest of men; agreeable to Jeremiah 23:28–29. God having there been reproving the false prophets that prophesied in his name and pretended that what they spake was his word, when indeed it was their own word, says, "The prophet that hath a dream, let him tell a dream; and he that hath my word, let him speak my word faithfully: what is the chaff to the wheat? saith the Lord. Is not my word like as a fire? saith the Lord: and like a hammer that breaketh the rock in pieces."

That we should expect such excellent divine things to be seen

2. If there be such a distinguishing excellency in divine things, it is rational to suppose that there may be such a thing as seeing it. What should hinder that it may be seen? It is no argument that there is no such distinguishing excellency, or that it cannot be seen, because some do not see it, though they may be discerning men in temporal matters. It is not rational to suppose, if there be any such excellency

in divine things, that wicked men should see it. Is it rational to suppose that those whose minds are full of spiritual pollution, and under the power of filthy lusts, should have any relish or sense of divine beauty or excellency; or that their minds should be susceptive of that light that is in its own nature so pure and heavenly? It need not seem at all strange that sin should so blind the mind, seeing that men's particular natural tempers and dispositions will so much blind them in secular matters; as when men's natural temper is melancholy, jealous, fearful, proud, or the like.

That this knowledge should be given by God alone

3. It is rational to suppose, that this knowledge should be given immediately by God, and not be obtained by natural means. Upon what account should it seem unreasonable that there should be any immediate communication between God and the creature? It is strange that men should make any matter of difficulty of it. Why should not he that made all things, still have something immediately to do with the things that he has made? Where lies the great difficulty, if we own the being of a God, and that he created all things out of nothing, of allowing some immediate influence of God on the creation still? And if it be reasonable to suppose it with respect to any part of the creation, it is especially so with respect to reasonable intelligent creatures; who are next to God in the gradation of the different orders of beings, and whose business is most immediately with God; and reason teaches that man was made to serve and glorify his Creator. And if it be rational to sup-

pose that God immediately communicates himself to man in any affair, it is in this. It is rational to suppose that God would reserve that knowledge and wisdom which is of such a divine and excellent nature, to be bestowed immediately by himself; and that it should not be left in the power of second causes.

Spiritual wisdom and grace is the highest and most excellent gift that ever God bestows on any creature: in this the highest excellency and perfection of a rational creature consists. It is also immensely the most important of all divine gifts: it is that wherein man's happiness consists, and that on which his everlasting welfare depends. How rational is it to suppose that God, however he has left lower gifts to second causes, and in some sort in their power, yet should reserve this most excellent, divine, and important of all divine communications, in his own hands, to be bestowed immediately by himself, as a thing too great for second causes to be concerned in? It is rational to suppose that this blessing should be immediately from God, for there is no gift or benefit that is in itself so nearly related to the divine nature. Nothing which the creature receives is so much a participation of the Deity: it is a kind of emanation of God's beauty, and is related to God as the light is to the sun. It is therefore congruous and fit, that when it is given of God, it should be immediately from himself, and by himself, according to his own sovereign will.

That this knowledge is directly given by God and not by natural reason

It is rational to suppose that it should be beyond man's power to obtain this light by the mere strength of natural reason; for it is not a thing that belongs to reason to see the beauty and loveliness of spiritual things; it is not a speculative thing, but depends on the sense of the heart.

Reason indeed is necessary in order to it, as it is by reason only that we are become the subjects of the means of it; which means I have already shown to be necessary in order to it, though they have not proper causal influence in the affair. It is by reason that we become possessed of a notion of those doctrines that are the subject matter of this divine light, or knowledge; and reason may many ways be indirectly and remotely an advantage to it. Reason also has to do in the acts that are immediately consequent on this discovery: for seeing the truth of religion hence is by reason; though it be but by one step, and the inference be immediate. So reason has to do in that accepting and trusting in Christ that is consequent on it.

But if we take *reason* strictly—not for the faculty of mental perception in general, but for ratiocination, or a power of inferring by arguments—the perceiving of spiritual beauty and excellency no more belongs to reason, than it belongs to the sense of feeling to perceive colors, or to the power of seeing to perceive the sweetness of food. It is out of reason's province to perceive the beauty or loveliness of anything: such a perception does not belong to that faculty. Reason's work is to perceive truth and not excellency. It is not ratiocination that gives men the perception of the beauty and amiableness of a countenance, though it may be many ways indirectly an advantage to it; yet it is no more reason that immediately perceives it, than it is reason that perceives the sweetness of honey: it depends on the sense of the heart. Reason may determine that a countenance is beautiful to others, it may determine that honey is sweet to others; but it will never give me a perception of sweetness.

CONCLUDING IMPROVEMENT

I will conclude with a very brief improvement of what has been said.

This doctrine leads us to reflect on God's goodness

First, this doctrine may lead us to reflect on the goodness of God, that has so ordered it, that a saving evidence of the truth of the gospel is such as is attainable by persons of mean capacities and advantages, as well as those that are of the greatest parts and learning. If the evidence of the gospel depended only on history, and such reasonings as learned men only are capable of, it would be above the reach of the greatest part of mankind. But persons with an ordinary degree of knowledge are capable, without a long and subtle train of reasoning, to see the divine excellency of the things of religion: they are capable of being taught by the Spirit of God, as well as learned men. The evidence that is this way obtained is vastly better and more satisfying than all that can be obtained by the arguings of those that are most learned, and greatest masters of reason. And babes are as capable of knowing these things as the wise and prudent; and they are often hid from these when they are revealed to those: "For ye see your calling, brethren, how that not many wise men after the flesh, not many mighty, not many noble are called. But God hath chosen the foolish things of the world" (1 Cor. 1:26–27).

This doctrine calls us to examine ourselves

Second, this doctrine may well put us upon examining ourselves, whether we have ever had this divine light let into our souls. If there be such a thing, doubtless it is of great importance whether we have thus been taught by the Spirit of God; whether the light of the glorious gospel of Christ, who is the image of God, hath shined unto us, giving us the light of the knowledge of the glory of God in the face of Jesus Christ; whether we have seen the Son, and believed on him, or have that faith of gospel-doctrines which arises from a spiritual sight of Christ.

All should seek this divine and supernatural light

Third, all may hence be exhorted, earnestly, to seek this spiritual light. To influence and move to it, the following things may be considered.

1. This is the most excellent and divine wisdom that any creature is capable of. It is more excellent than any human learning; it is far more excellent than all the knowledge of the greatest philosophers or statesmen. Yea, the least glimpse of the glory of God in the face of Christ doth more exalt and ennoble the soul, than all the knowledge of those that have the greatest speculative understanding in divinity without grace. This knowledge has the most noble object that can be, viz., the divine glory and excellency of

God and Christ. The knowledge of these objects is that wherein consists the most excellent knowledge of the angels, yea, of God himself.

2. This knowledge is that which is above all others sweet and joyful. Men have a great deal of pleasure in human knowledge, in studies of natural things; but this is nothing to that joy which arises from this divine light shining into the soul. This light gives a view of those things that are immensely the most exquisitely beautiful and capable of delighting the eye of the understanding. This spiritual light is the dawning of the light of glory in the heart. There is nothing so powerful as this to support persons in affliction, and to give the mind peace and brightness in this stormy and dark world.

3. This light is such as effectually influences the inclination and changes the nature of the soul. It assimilates our nature to the divine nature, and changes the soul into an image of the glory that is beheld: "But we all with open face, beholding as in a glass the glory of the Lord, are changed into the same image, from glory to glory, even as by the Spirit of the Lord" (2 Cor. 3:18). This knowledge will wean from the world, and raise the inclination to heavenly things. It will turn the heart to God as the fountain of good, and to choose him for the only portion. This light, and this light only, will bring the soul to a saving close with Christ. It conforms the heart to the gospel, mortifies its enmity and opposition against the scheme of salvation therein revealed: it causes the heart to embrace the joyful tidings, and entirely to adhere to, and acquiesce

in the revelation of Christ as our Savior: it causes the whole soul to accord and symphonize with it, admitting with entire credit and respect, cleaving to it with full inclination and affection; and it effectually disposes the soul to give up itself entirely to Christ.

4. This light, and this only, has its fruit in an eternal holiness of life. No merely notional or speculative understanding of the doctrines of religion will ever bring to this. But this light, as it reaches the bottom of the heart, and changes the nature, so it will effectually dispose to a universal obedience. It shows God as worthy to be obeyed and served. It draws forth the heart in a sincere love to God, which is the only principle of a true, gracious, and universal obedience; and it convinces of the reality of those glorious rewards that God has promised to those that obey him.

STUDY QUESTIONS

1. Edwards closes this sermon by citing the excellencies and advantages of the divine and supernatural light. Summarize these in your own words. Which of these would you like to see more of in your life? What might your life begin to look like if these benefits were more consistently present?

2. Edwards says that God alone gives this light, as Scripture and reason show; yet he counsels us to "seek this spiritual light." How do you suppose one would go about doing that? What is the role of the mind in this effort? Of the heart? How can you tell from looking at another person's

life that he or she is a true and earnest seeker of divine and supernatural light?

3. Edwards variously describes this divine and supernatural light as grace and truth, the doctrines of true religion, divine things, the glory of God in the face of Jesus Christ, knowing and seeing God, and so forth. Suppose you were to try to explain the light Edwards writes about to another person. What would you say about it? How would you try to impress that person with the excellencies and advantages of this light and of the importance of seeking it?

4. Take a moment to reflect on the degree to which you experience this knowledge of the glory of God in the face of Jesus Christ in your life, day by day. Use the scale below. Circle the number that best indicates your sense of the degree of your experience of divine and supernatural light:

1 2 3 4 5 6 7 8 9 10

hardly at all   *to a very high degree*

Why did you circle the number you did?

5. Review the goals you set for yourself at the outset of this study. Have you made any progress in realizing those goals? In what ways? How do you hope to grow further as we continue our study of Edwards on growing in God's Spirit?

❈ *Part 2* ❈

CHRISTIAN KNOWLEDGE

❧ Chapter 4 ❧
TIME TO GET GROWING

While only God can impart that divine and supernatural light that leads to growing in God's Spirit, we have a duty to seek the light, primarily by recourse to the Word of God in Scripture. In the first sermon Edwards emphasized the role of God in the process of Christian growth; in this sermon he will help us to take up our responsibility for becoming more like the Lord. In this introductory section Edwards sets his text in its biblical and historical context, declares his proposition, and outlines what is to follow.

❧

HEBREWS 5:12

For when for the time ye ought to be teachers, ye have need that one teach you again which be the first principles of the oracles of God; and are become such as have need of milk, and not of strong meat.

THE APOSTLE'S COMPLAINT

These words are a complaint, which the apostle makes against the Christian Hebrews, for their want of such proficiency in the knowledge of the doctrines and mysteries of religion, as might have been expected of them. The apostle complains that they had not made that progress in their acquaintance with the things taught in the oracles of God, which they ought to have made. And he means to reprove them, not merely for their deficiency in *spiritual* and *experimental*[1] knowledge of divine things, but for their deficiency in *doctrinal* acquaintance with the principles of religion, and the truths of Christian divinity; as is evident by the manner in which the apostle introduces this reproof.

The occasion of his introducing it is this: in the next verse but one preceding, he mentions Christ as being "called of God an high priest after the order of Melchisedec." In the Old Testament, the oracles of God, Melchizedek was held forth as an eminent type of Christ; and the account we there have of him contains many gospel mysteries. These mysteries the apostle was willing to point out to the Christian Hebrews; but he apprehended that through their weakness in knowledge, they would not understand him; and therefore breaks off for the present from saying anything about Melchizedek, thus (v. 11), "Of whom we have many things to say, and hard to be uttered; seeing ye are all dull of hearing"; i.e., there are many things concerning Melchizedek which contain wonderful gospel mysteries, and which I would take notice of to you, were it not that I am afraid, that through your dullness and backwardness in understanding these things, you would only be

1. With other Puritan writers, Edwards used the word *experimental* to mean something like "experiential," or "real," or "relating to experience."

puzzled and confounded by my discourse, and so receive no benefit; and that it would be too hard for you, as meat that is too strong.

Then come in the words of the text: "For when for the time ye ought to be teachers, ye have need that one teach you again which be the first principles of the oracles of God; and are become such as have need of milk, and not of strong meat." As much as to say, Indeed it might have been expected of you, that you should have known enough of the Holy Scriptures, to be able to understand and digest such mysteries: but it is not so with you. The apostle speaks of their proficiency in such knowledge as is conveyed by *human* teaching: as appears by that expression, "When for the time ye ought to be teachers," which includes not only a practical and experimental, but also a *doctrinal, knowledge* of the truths and mysteries of religion.

DEGREES OF CHRISTIAN KNOWLEDGE

Of milk and meat

Again, the apostle speaks of such knowledge, whereby Christians are enabled to understand those things in divinity which are more abstruse and difficult to be understood, and which require great skill in things of this nature. This is more fully expressed in the next two verses: "For every one that useth milk, is unskillful in the word of righteousness; for he is a babe. But strong meat belongeth to them that are of full age, even those who, by reason of use, have their senses exercised to discern both good and evil." It is such knowledge, that proficiency in it shall carry persons beyond the first principles of religion. As here: "Ye have need that one teach you again which be the first principles of the oracles of God." Therefore the apostle, in the beginning of the next chapter, advises them to leave the first principles of the doctrine of Christ, and to go on unto perfection.

How their fault in this appears

We may observe that the fault of this defect appears, in that they had not made *proficiency* according to their time. For the time, they ought to have been teachers. As they were Christians, their business was to learn and gain Christian knowledge. They were scholars in the school of Christ; and if they had improved their time in learning, as they ought to have done, they might, by the time when the apostle wrote, have been fit to be teachers in this school. To whatever business one is devoted, it may be expected that his perfection in it shall be answerable to the time he has had to learn and perfect himself. Christians should not always remain babes, but should grow in Christian knowledge; and leaving the food of babes, they should learn to digest strong meat.

THE CHRISTIAN'S CALLING

DOCTRINE: Every Christian should make a business of endeavoring to grow in knowledge in divinity. This is indeed esteemed the business of divines[2] and ministers: it is commonly thought to be their work, by the study of the Scriptures, and other instructive books, to gain knowledge; and most seem to think that it may be left to them, as what belongeth not to others. But if the apostle had entertained this notion, he would never have blamed the Christian Hebrews for not having acquired knowledge enough to be teachers. Or if he had thought that this concerned Christians in general only as a thing by the bye, and that their time should not in a considerable measure be taken up with this business; he never would have so much blamed them, that their proficiency in knowledge had not been answerable to the time which they had had to learn.

In handling this subject, I shall show—what is intended by *divinity*—what kind of *knowledge* in divinity is intended—*why* knowledge in divinity is *necessary*.

And why all Christians should make a business of endeavoring to *grow* in this knowledge.

STUDY QUESTIONS

1. Edwards considered that every Christian who was not able to see the many "gospel mysteries" that are embedded in the Old Testament story and teachings about Melchizedek was beset by "dullness and backwardness in understanding." In this he was only echoing the writer of the Book of Hebrews. Suppose you were charged with sharing the

2. Theologians.

gospel with someone, using only the story of Melchizedek in Genesis 14:17–24 and other Old Testament texts. Would you be able to derive sufficient "gospel mysteries" from just this much of Scripture to explain the gospel to another person? Where would you place yourself on the "dullness and backwardness in understanding" scale?

2. Edwards uses the terms *divinity* and *divine knowledge* or *Christian knowledge* interchangeably. What does he seem to mean by these ideas? What is your understanding of how such knowledge relates to the divine and supernatural light discussed in the first sermon? To the process of Christian growth?

3. He says that all Christians are "scholars in the school of Christ." Suppose you had a child who was a full-time college student. What kinds of expectations would you hold out for that child? If you could inspect his or her daily activities, what would you expect to see? As "disciples"— that is, *learners* of Christ—what should we expect of ourselves, we who are "scholars in the school of Christ"?

4. How would you be able to tell when one of Christ's scholars was stuck in baby food and needed to move on? Does Edwards seem to think there is a relationship between time invested in knowing the Lord and expectations of Christian growth? What might that relationship be? How much of your time each week is devoted to "mak[ing] a business of endeavoring to grow in knowledge in divinity"?

5. How would you summarize the business that occupies a typical week in your life? How much time is spent at your

job? Taking care of your home or family? Pursuing interests and avocations? Watching television or engaging in other diversions? If someone were to study your life carefully for a couple of weeks, what would he conclude is the "business" of your life? Why? What would your life look like if you, following Edwards's advice, began more to "make a business of endeavoring to grow in knowledge in divinity"?

✼ Chapter 5 ✼

THE NATURE AND NECESSITY OF DIVINITY

Edwards explains what he means by divinity, or, Christian doctrine. He shows that we must not be satisfied with mere "head knowledge" as we study the Word of God, but we must labor to bring head and heart together in the task of knowing the things of the Lord. This is the way to a life of loving God and others. Knowledge of divinity is the proper business of people who have been endowed with reason in order that they might understand and embrace the things of God revealed in his Word.

DIVINITY AS THE SCIENCE OF RELIGION

Various definitions have been given of this subject by those who have treated on it. I shall not now stand to inquire which, according to the rules of art, is the most accurate definition; but shall so define or describe it, as I think has the greatest tendency to convey a proper notion of it. It is that science or doctrine which comprehends all those truths and rules which concern the great business of religion.

Divinity as doctrine

There are various kinds of arts and sciences taught and learned in the schools, which are conversant about various objects; about the works of nature in general, as philosophy; or the visible heavens, as astronomy; or the sea, as navigation; or the earth, as geography; or the body of man, as physic[1] and anatomy; or the soul of a man, with regard to its natural powers and qualities, as logic and pneumatology; or about human government, as politics and jurisprudence. But one science, or kind of knowledge and doctrine, is above all the rest: as it treats concerning God and the great business of religion.[2] *Divinity* is not learned, as other sciences, merely by the improvement of man's natural reason, but is taught by God himself in a book full of instruction, which he hath given us for that end. This is the rule which God hath given to the world to be their guide in searching after this kind of knowledge, and is a summary of all things of this nature needful for us to know. Upon this account divinity is rather called a doctrine, than an art or science.

The source of divinity

Indeed there is what is called *natural religion*. There are many truths concerning God, and our duty to him, which

1. Medicine.
2. By "religion" Edwards means Christianity.

are evident by the light of nature. But *Christian divinity,* properly so called, is not evident by the light of nature; it depends on revelation. Such are our circumstances now in our fallen state, that nothing which it is needful for us to know concerning God is manifest by the light of nature in the manner in which it is necessary for us to know it. For the knowledge of no truth in divinity is of significance to us any otherwise than as it some way or other belongs to the gospel scheme, or as it relates to a Mediator. But the light of nature teaches us no truth in this matter. Therefore it cannot be said, that we come to the knowledge of any part of Christian truth by the light of nature. It is only the Word of God, contained in the Old and New Testament, which teaches us Christian divinity.

The subject matter of divinity

This comprehends all that is taught in the Scriptures, and so all that we need to know, or is to be known, concerning God and Jesus Christ, concerning our duty to God, and our happiness in God. Divinity is commonly defined, *the doctrine of living to God;* and by some who seem to be more accurate, *the doctrine of living to God by Christ.* It comprehends all Christian doctrines as they are in Jesus, and all Christian rules directing us in living to God by Christ. There is no one doctrine, no promise, no rule, but what some way or other relates to the Christian and divine life, or our living to God by Christ. They all relate to this, in two respects, viz., as they tend to promote our living to God here in this world, in a life of faith and holiness, and also as they tend to bring us to a life of perfect holiness and happiness, in the full enjoyment of God hereafter.

THE NATURE OF DIVINITY

Two aspects of divinity

There are two kinds of knowledge of divine truth, viz., *speculative* and *practical,* or in other terms, *natural* and *spiritual.* The former remains only in the head. No other faculty but the understanding is concerned in it. It consists in having a natural or rational knowledge of the things of religion, or such a knowledge as is to be obtained by the natural exercise of our own faculties, without any special illumination of the Spirit of God. The latter rests not entirely in the head, or in the speculative ideas of things; but the heart is concerned in it: it principally consists in the sense of the heart. The mere intellect, without the will or the inclination, is not the seat of it. And it may not only be called seeing, but feeling or tasting. Thus there is a difference between having a right speculative notion of the doctrines contained in the Word of God, and having a due sense of them in the heart. In the former consists the speculative or natural knowledge, in the latter consists the spiritual or practical knowledge of them.

Neither of these is intended in the doctrine exclusively of the other: but it is intended that we should seek the former *in order* to the latter. The latter, or the spiritual and practical, is of the greatest importance; for a speculative without a spiritual knowledge is to no purpose, but to make our condemnation greater. Yet a speculative knowledge is also of infinite importance in this respect, that without it we can have no spiritual or practical knowledge.

The relationship between the two aspects of divinity

I have already shown, that the apostle speaks not only of a spiritual knowledge, but of such as can be acquired and communicated from one to another. Yet it is not to be thought that he means this exclusively of the other. But he would have the Christian Hebrews seek the one in order to the other. Therefore the former is first and most *directly* intended; it is intended that Christians should, by reading and other proper means, seek a good *rational knowledge* of the things of divinity: while the latter is more *indirectly* intended, since it is to be sought by the other.

But I proceed to the usefulness and necessity of the knowledge of divine truths.

THE NECESSITY OF DIVINITY

No teaching without learning

There is no other way by which any means of grace whatsoever can be of any benefit, but by knowledge. All teaching is in vain without learning. Therefore the preaching of the gospel would be wholly to no purpose, if it conveyed no knowledge to the mind. There is an order of men which Christ has appointed on purpose to be teachers in his church. But they teach in vain, if no knowledge in these things is gained by their teaching. It is impossible that

---

their teaching and preaching should be a means of grace, or of any good in the hearts of their hearers, any otherwise than by knowledge imparted to the understanding. Otherwise it would be of as much benefit to the auditory,[3] if the minister should preach in some unknown tongue. All the difference is that preaching in a known tongue conveys something to the understanding, which preaching in an unknown tongue doth not. On this account, such preaching must be unprofitable. In such things men receive nothing when they understand nothing; and are not at all edified, unless some knowledge be conveyed, agreeable to the apostle's arguing (I Cor. 14:2–6).

No speech can be a means of grace, but by conveying knowledge. Otherwise the speech is as much lost as if there had been no man there, and if he that spoke had spoken only into the air; as it follows in the passage just quoted, verses 6–10. God deals with man as with a rational creature; and when faith is in exercise, it is not about something he knows not what. Therefore hearing is absolutely necessary to faith; because hearing is necessary to understanding: "How shall they believe in him of whom they have not heard?" (Rom. 10:14). In like manner, there can be no love without knowledge. It is not according to the nature of the human soul to love an object which is entirely unknown. The heart cannot be set upon an object of which there is no idea in the understanding. The reasons which induce the soul to love, must first be understood, before they can have a reasonable influence on the heart.

3. Those listening to preaching or teaching.

The Bible and knowledge

God hath given us the Bible, which is a book of instructions. But this book can be of no manner of profit to us any otherwise than as it conveys some knowledge to the mind: it can profit us no more than if it were written in the Chinese or Tartarian language, of which we know not one word. So the sacraments of the gospel can have a proper effect no other way, than by conveying some knowledge. They represent certain things by visible signs. And what is the end of signs, but to convey some knowledge of things signified? Such is the nature of man, that no object can come at the heart but through the door of understanding: and there can be no spiritual knowledge of that of which there is not first a rational knowledge. It is impossible that anyone should see the truth or excellency of any doctrine of the gospel, who knows not what that doctrine is. A man cannot see the wonderful excellency and love of Christ in doing such and such things for sinners, unless his understanding be first informed how those things were done. He cannot have a taste of the sweetness and excellency of divine truth, unless he first have a notion that there is such a thing.

The importance of divinity

Without a knowledge in divinity, none would differ from the most ignorant and barbarous heathens. The heathens remain in gross darkness, because they are not instructed, and have not obtained knowledge of divine truths.

If men have no knowledge of these things, the faculty of reason in him will be wholly in vain. The faculty of reason and understanding was given for *actual* understanding and knowledge. If a man have not actual knowledge, the faculty or capacity of knowing is of no use to him. And if he have actual knowledge, yet if he be destitute of the knowledge of those things which are the last end of his being, and for the sake of the knowledge of which he had more understanding given him than the beasts; then still his faculty of reason is in vain; he might as well have been a beast as a man. But divine subjects are the things to know which we had the faculty of reason given us. They are the things which appertain to the end of our being, and to the great business for which we are made. Therefore a man cannot have his faculty of understanding to any good purpose, further than he hath knowledge of divine truth.

So that this kind of knowledge is absolutely necessary. Other kinds of knowledge may be very useful. Some other sciences, such as astronomy, natural philosophy, and geography, may be very excellent in their kind. But knowledge of this divine science is infinitely more useful and important than that of all other sciences whatever.

STUDY QUESTIONS

1. Edwards uses the term *divinity* the way we might use the term *theology*. Some people might find "theology" somewhat off-putting. Why do you think this is so? Yet look at Romans 1:18–21 and Ecclesiastes 3:11. Based on these

passages, how can you see that it is possible to say that everyone is a theologian? In that case, what is the difference between a good theologian and a bad one? What is the difference between a good theologian and a better one?

2. Edwards argues that true divinity—true knowledge of God—is not just a matter of the head. As he argued in his first sermon, head and heart must come together if true knowledge of divinity is to be achieved. What is the difference between these two? Why is each important in the learning process? What dangers can arise from emphasizing the head to the exclusion of the heart? From emphasizing the heart to the exclusion of the head?

3. Edwards maintains that much useful knowledge can come from other disciplines and studies—the sciences and other fields of knowledge. Given what we read in Psalm 19:1–6 and Romans 1:18–21, why would this be so? Nevertheless, what makes divinity so much more important than any of these other fields of study? How should we think about the relationship between divinity and other sciences?

4. Love is the end of all study of divinity, according to Edwards. This would seem to be in accord with what Jesus says in Matthew 22:34–40, what Paul intimates in I Timothy 1:5 (cf. Gal. 5:6), and what John claims in I John 5:1–3. In your experience, to what extent have the preachers and teachers under whom you have sat emphasized that all their instruction must issue in love for God and neighbors if it is to be truly learned? Do you think that the contemporary Christian community, with all our many

Christian educational activities, views learning like this? Explain.

5. How would you explain to another person what Edwards means by "the great business for which we are made"? What is the relationship between our calling as disciples of Christ and a disciplined life of gaining knowledge of divinity? What kinds of things tend to get in the way of our prosecuting this "great business" as dutifully as we might? What might you be able to do in your life in order to make more time available for this "great business"?

❦ *Chapter 6* ❦

THE BUSINESS OF CHRISTIAN GROWTH (I)

Edwards begins an argument for the importance of every believer devoting himself to the task of acquiring divine knowledge. We must not be merely casual or cavalier—"by the bye," as Edwards says—about this calling; instead, understanding that this is why reason has been granted us, and seeing the riches of divine truth and the lengths God has gone to make his truth known to us, we should take up this calling as a most important part of our lives day by day.

Christians ought not to content themselves with such degrees of knowledge of divinity as they have already obtained. It should not satisfy them, as they know as much as is absolutely necessary to salvation, but should seek to make progress.

This endeavor to make progress in such knowledge ought not to be attended to as a thing by the bye, but all Christians should make a *business* of it. They should look upon it as a part of their *daily* business, and no small part of it either. It should be attended to as a considerable part of their high calling. For,

The Stewardship of Reason

1. Our business should doubtless much consist in employing those faculties by which we are distinguished from the beasts, about those things which are the main end of those faculties.

The reason for reason

The reason why we have faculties superior to those of the brutes given us is, that we are indeed designed for a superior employment. That which the Creator intended should be our main employment is something above what he intended the beast for, and therefore hath given us superior powers. Therefore, without doubt, it should be a considerable part of our business to improve those superior faculties. But the faculty by which we are chiefly distinguished from the brutes is the faculty of understanding. It follows then, that we should make it our chief business to improve this faculty, and should by no means prosecute it as a business by the bye. For us to make the improvement of this faculty a business by the bye, is in effect for us to make the faculty of understanding itself a *by-faculty*, if I may so speak, a faculty of less importance than others: whereas indeed it is the highest faculty we have.

The superiority of understanding over sensation

But we cannot make a business of the improvement of our intellectual faculty, any otherwise than by making a business of improving ourselves in actual knowledge. So that those who make not this very much their business, but instead of improving their understanding to acquire knowledge, are chiefly devoted to their inferior power—to please their senses, and gratify their animal appetites—not only behave themselves in a manner not becoming Christians, but also act as if they had forgotten that they are men, and that God hath set them above the brutes, by giving them understanding.

God hath given to man some things in common with the brutes, as his outward senses, his bodily appetites, a capacity of bodily pleasure and pain, and other animal faculties: and some things he hath given him superior to the brutes, the chief of which is a faculty of understanding and reason. Now God never gave man these faculties to be subject to those which he hath in common with the brutes. This would be a great confusion, and equivalent to making man a servant to the beasts. On the contrary, he has given those inferior powers to be employed in subserviency to man's understanding; and therefore it must be a great part of man's principal business to improve his understanding by acquiring knowledge. If so, then it will follow, that it should be a main part of his business to improve his understanding in acquiring *divine* knowledge, or the knowledge of the things of divinity: for the knowledge of these things is the principal end of this faculty. God gave man the faculty of understanding, chiefly, that he might understand divine things.

Reason meant for divine knowledge

The wiser heathens were sensible that the main business of man was the improvement and exercise of his understanding. But they knew not the object about which the understanding should be chiefly employed. That science which many of them thought should chiefly employ the understanding, was philosophy; and accordingly they made it their chief business to study it. But we who enjoy the light of the gospel are more happy; we are not left, as to this particular, in the dark. God hath told us about what things we should chiefly employ our understandings, having given us a book full of divine instructions, holding forth many glorious objects about which all rational creatures should chiefly employ their understandings. These instructions are accommodated to persons of all capacities and conditions, and proper to be studied, not only by men of learning, but by persons of every character, learned and unlearned, young and old, men and women. Therefore the acquisition of knowledge in these things should be a main business of all who have the advantage of enjoying the Holy Scriptures.

THE EXCELLENCY OF DIVINE TRUTH

2. The truths of divinity are superlative excellency, and are worthy that all should make a business of endeavoring to grow in knowledge of them.

The subject matter of divinity

They are as much above those things which are treated of in other sciences, as heaven is above the earth. God himself, the eternal Three in one, is the chief object of this science; and next Jesus Christ, as God-man and Mediator, and the glorious work of redemption, the most glorious work that ever was wrought: then the great things of the heavenly world, the glorious and eternal inheritance purchased by Christ and promised in the gospel; the work of the Holy Spirit of God on the hearts of men; our duty to God, and the way in which we ourselves may become like angels, and like God himself in our measure. All these are objects of this science.

Divine truth a great treasure

Such things as these have been the main subject of the study of the holy patriarchs, prophets, and apostles, and the most excellent men that ever existed; and they are also the subject of study to the angels in heaven (1 Peter 1:10–12). They are so excellent and worthy to be known, that the knowledge of them will richly pay for all the pains and labor of an earnest seeking of it. If there were a great treasure of gold and pearls accidentally found, and opened with such circumstances that all might have as much as they could gather; would not everyone think it worth his while to make a business of gathering while it should last? But the treasure of divine knowledge, which is contained in the Scriptures, and is provided for everyone to gather as much of it as he can, is far more rich than any one of gold and pearls. How busy are all sorts of men, all over the world, in getting riches! But this knowledge is a far better kind of riches than that after which they so diligently and laboriously pursue.

DIVINE KNOWLEDGE THE BUSINESS OF ALL CHRISTIANS

3. Divine truths not only concern ministers, but are of infinite importance to all Christians.

The eternal significance of divine knowledge: the doctrines of God

It is not with the doctrines of divinity as it is with the doctrines of philosophy and other sciences. These last are generally speculative points, which are of little concern in human life; and it very little alters the case as to our temporal or spiritual interests, whether we know them or not. Philosophers differ about them, some being of one opinion, and others of another. And while they are engaged in warm disputes about them, others may well leave them to dispute among themselves, without troubling their heads much about them; it being of little concern to them, whether the one or the other be in the right. But it is not thus in matters of divinity. The doctrines of this nearly[1] concern everyone. They are about those things which relate to every man's eternal salvation and happiness. The common people cannot say, "Let us leave these matters to ministers and divines; let them dispute them out among themselves as they can; they concern not us": for they are of infinite importance to every man. Those doctrines which relate to the essence, attributes, and sub-

1. Not in the sense of "almost," but "closely."

sistencies of God, concern all; as it is of infinite importance to common people, as well as ministers, to
know what kind of being God is. For he is a Being who
hath made us all, "in whom we live, and move, and have
our being"; who is the Lord of all; the Being to whom
we are all accountable; is the last end of our being, and
the only fountain of our happiness.

The doctrines of Christ and the Spirit

The doctrines also which relate to Jesus Christ and his
mediation, his incarnation, his life and death, his resurrection and ascension, his sitting at the right hand of the
Father, his satisfaction and intercession, infinitely concern
common people as well as divines. They stand in as much
need of this Savior, and of an interest in his person and
offices, and the things which he hath done and suffered,
as ministers and divines. The same may be said of the doctrines which relate to the manner of a sinner's justification, or the way in which he becomes interested in the
mediation of Christ. They equally concern all; for all
stand in equal necessity of justification before God. That
eternal condemnation, to which we are all naturally ex-
posed, is equally dreadful. So with respect to those doctrines which relate to the work of the Spirit of God on the
heart, in the application of redemption in our effectual
calling and sanctification, all are equally concerned in
them. There is no doctrine of divinity whatever, which
doth not some way or other concern the eternal interest of
every Christian.

WHAT LENGTHS GOD HAS GONE TO INSTRUCT US

4. We may argue in favor of the same position, from the great things which God hath done in order to give us instruction in these things.

The gift of Scripture

As to other sciences, he hath left us to ourselves, to the light of our own reason. But divine things being of infinitely greater importance to us, he hath not left us to an uncertain guide; but hath himself given us a revelation of truth in these matters, and hath done very great things to convey and confirm it to us; raising up many prophets in different ages, immediately inspiring them with this Holy Spirit, and confirming their doctrine with innumerable miracles or wonderful works out of the established course of nature. Yea, he raised up a succession of prophets, which was upheld for several ages.

It was very much for this end that God separated the people of Israel, in so wonderful a manner, from all other people, and kept them separate; that to them he might commit the oracles of God, and that from them they might be communicated to the world. He hath also often sent angels to bring divine instructions to men; and hath often himself appeared in miraculous symbols or representations of his presence: and now in these last days hath sent his own Son into the world, to be his great prophet, to teach us divine truth (Heb. 1:1, etc.). God hath given us a book of divine instructions, which contains the sum of divinity. Now these things God hath done, not only for the instruction of ministers and men of learning; but for the instruction of all men, of all sorts, learned and unlearned, men, women, and children. And certainly if God doth such great things to *teach* us, we ought to do something to *learn*.

The necessity earnestly to prosecute this business

God giving instruction to men in these things is not a business by the bye; but what he hath undertaken and prosecuted in a course of great and wonderful dispensations, as an affair in which his heart hath been greatly engaged; which is sometimes in Scripture signified by the expression of God's rising early to teach us, and to send us prophets and teachers: "Since that day that your fathers came forth out of the land of Egypt, unto this day, I have even sent unto you all my servants the prophets, daily rising up early, and sending them" (Jer. 7:25). And, "I spake unto you, rising up early, and speaking" (v. 13). This is a figurative speech, signifying that God hath done this as a business of great importance, in which he took great care, and had his heart much engaged; because persons are wont to rise early to prosecute such business as they are earnestly engaged in. If God hath been so engaged in teaching, certainly we should not be negligent in learning; but should make growing in knowledge a great part of the business of our lives.

STUDY QUESTIONS

1. Edwards's use of the term *business* to categorize the study of divine truth is an interesting choice of words, particularly in our day. Typically, how do people tend to think about their "business"? What sorts of things characterize their approach to "business"?

2. Don't you love the way Edwards uses the phrase "by the bye" to categorize what our approach to divine knowledge must *not* be? What do you suppose he had in mind by this term? What would a person look like who maintained such a casual or cavalier approach to acquiring divine truth? Do you think most Christians today are more "businesslike" or "by the bye" about their pursuit of the knowledge of divine truth? Explain.

3. Edwards says that our reason, or understanding, has been given to us to separate us from the animals. When we put reason on the shelf and instead live our lives solely for the gratification of our appetites, we have, in effect, forfeited our humanity. How might you tell if a person were more devoted to satisfying his or her appetites than using understanding to acquire divine knowledge? What would such a person look like? How would his or her time be allotted to each of these matters? What would his or her priorities look like?

4. Edwards shows that God has taken a very "businesslike" approach to making divine truth available to us. He has gone to great lengths to provide for us. Summarize his ar-

guments here. Have you ever thought about the process of God's giving his Word in this way? Does understanding the great lengths God has gone to provide us with his Word—and to preserve it for us through all these centuries—affect your attitude toward Scripture in any way?

5. Edwards insists over and over that divine truth is important to every Christian, and not just to theologians and ministers. Do you think most Christians today would agree with Edwards on this point? Why or why not? What should be the role of pastors and teachers in helping to press this point on the members of their churches? How might church members encourage their pastors and teachers in doing so?

❖ *Chapter 7* ❖

THE BUSINESS OF CHRISTIAN GROWTH (2)

Edwards continues his argument about the importance of all Christians devoting themselves to the business of growing in Christian knowledge. The great quantity of revelation in Scripture, the inadequacy of our knowledge at any time, the nature of our calling, God's appointment of teachers and learners, and the need of striving for excellence in divine truth all argue for each believer taking up this endeavor with diligence and devotion.

❖

THE GREAT BULK OF SCRIPTURE

5. It may be argued from the abundance of the instructions which God hath given us, from the largeness of that book which God hath given to teach us divinity, and from the great variety that is therein contained.

The sheer quantity of revelation in Scripture

Much was taught by Moses of old, which we have transmitted down to us; after that, other books were from time to time added; much is taught us by David and Solomon; and the prophets: yet God did not think all this enough, but after this sent Christ and his apostles, by whom there is added a great and excellent treasure to that holy book, which is to be our rule in the study of this important subject.

This book was written for the use of all; all are directed to search the Scriptures: John 5:39, "Search the Scriptures, for in them ye think ye have eternal life; and they are they that testify of me"; and Isaiah 34:16, "Seek ye out of the book of the Lord, and read." They that read and understand are pronounced blessed: "Blessed is he that readeth, and they that understand the words of this prophecy" (Rev. 1:3). If this be true of that particular book of the *Revelation,* much more is it true of the Bible in general. Nor is it to be believed that God would have given instructions in such abundance, if he had intended that receiving instruction should be only a bye concern with us.

THE ABUNDANCE OF SCRIPTURE GIVEN IN ORDER TO BE UNDERSTOOD

It is to be considered, that all those abundant instructions which are contained in the Scriptures were written that they might be understood: otherwise they are not instructions. That which is not given that the learner may understand it, is not given for the learner's instruction; unless we endeavor to grow in the knowledge of divinity, a very great part of those instructions will to us be in vain; for we can receive benefit by no more of the Scriptures than we understand. We have reason to bless God that he hath given us such various and plentiful instruction in his Word; but we shall be hypocritical in so doing, if we after all content ourselves with but little of this instruction.

When God hath opened a very large treasure before us, for the supply of our wants, and we thank him that he hath given us so much; if at the same time we be willing to remain destitute of the greatest part of it, because we are too lazy to gather it, this will not show the sincerity of our thankfulness. We are now under much greater advantages to acquire knowledge in divinity, than the people of God were of old, because since that time the canon of Scripture is much increased. But if we be negligent of our advantages, we may be never the better for them, and may remain with as little knowledge as they.

ALWAYS ROOM TO LEARN MORE

6. However diligent we apply ourselves, there is room enough to increase our knowledge in divine truth.

No excuses!

None have this excuse to make for not diligently applying themselves to gain knowledge in divinity, that they already know all; nor can they make this excuse, that they have no need diligently to apply themselves, in order to know all that is to be known. None can excuse themselves for want of business in which to employ themselves. There is room enough to employ ourselves forever in this divine science, with the utmost application. Those who have applied themselves most closely, have studied the longest, and have made the greatest attainments in this knowledge, know but little of what is to be known. The subject is inexhaustible. That divine Being, who is the main subject of this science, is infinite, and there is no end of the glory of his perfections. His works at the same time are wonderful, and cannot be found out to perfection: especially the work of redemption, about which the science of divinity is chiefly conversant, is full of unsearchable wonders.

A subject for a lifetime of study

The Word of God, which is given for our instruction in divinity, contains enough in it to employ us to the end of our lives, and then we shall leave enough uninvestigated to employ the heads of the ablest divines to the end of the world. The psalmist found an end to the things that are human; but he could never find an end to what is contained in the Word of God: "I have seen an end to all perfection; but thy command is exceeding broad" (Ps. 119:96). There is enough in this divine science to employ the understandings of saints and angels to all eternity.

TO EXCEL IN OUR CALLING

7. It doubtless concerns everyone to endeavor to excel in the knowledge of things which pertain to his profession, or principal calling.

Called to live for God

If it concerns men to excel in anything, or in any wisdom or knowledge at all, it certainly concerns them to excel in the affairs of their main profession and work. But the calling and work of every Christian is to live to God. This is said to be his *high calling* (Phil. 3:14). This is the business, and, if I may so speak, the *trade* of a Christian, his main work. No business should be done by a Christian, but as it is some way or other a part of this. Therefore certainly the Christian should endeavor to be well acquainted with those things which belong to this work, that he may fulfill it, and be thoroughly furnished to it.

An analogy from life

It becomes one who is called to be a soldier, to excel in the art of war. It becomes a mariner, to excel in the art of navigation. It becomes a physician, to excel in the knowledge of those things which pertain to the art of physic. So it becomes all such as profess to be Christians, to devote themselves to the practice of Christianity, to endeavor to excel in the knowledge of divinity.

GOD'S APPOINTMENTS TO THIS GREAT END

8. It may be argued, hence, that God hath appointed an order of men for this end, to assist persons in gaining knowledge in these things.

The gift of teachers

He hath appointed them to be teachers (1 Cor. 12:28), and God hath set some in the church; first apostles, secondarily prophets, thirdly teachers (Eph. 4:11–12). "He gave some apostles, some prophets, some evangelists, some pastors and teachers, for the perfecting of the saints, for the work of the ministry, for the edifying of the body of Christ." If God hath set them to be teachers, making that their business, then he hath made it their business to impart knowledge. But what kind of knowledge? Not the knowledge of philosophy, or of human laws, or of mechanical arts, but of divinity.

Called to be learners

If God have made it the business of some to be teachers, it will follow, that he hath made it the business of others to be learners; for teachers and learners are correlates, one of which was never intended to be without the other. God hath never made it the duty of some to take pains to teach those who are not obliged to take pains to learn. He hath not commanded ministers to spend themselves, in order to impart knowledge to those who are not obliged to apply themselves to receive it.

The name by which Christians are commonly called in the New Testament is *disciples,* the signification of which word is *scholars* or *learners.* All Christians are put into the school of Christ, where their business is to learn, or receive knowledge from Christ, their common master and teacher, and from those inferior teachers appointed by him to instruct in his name.

GOD WILLS THAT ALL CHRISTIANS SHOULD LEARN

9. God hath in the Scriptures plainly revealed it to be his will, that all Christians should diligently endeavor to excel in the knowledge of divine things.

All Christians to be enriched in knowledge

It is the revealed will of God, that Christians should not only have some knowledge of things of this nature, but that they should be *enriched with all knowledge:* "I thank my God always on your behalf, for the grace of God that is given you by Jesus Christ, that in every thing ye are enriched by him, in all utterance, and in *all knowledge*" (1 Cor. 1:4–5). So the apostle earnestly prayed, that the Christian Philippians might abound more and more, not only in love, but in Christian *knowledge:* Philippians 1:9, "And this I pray, that your love may abound yet more and more in *knowledge,* and in *all judgment.*" So the apostle Peter advises to give all diligence to "add to faith virtue, and to virtue *knowledge*" (2 Peter 1:5).

Rest not in fundamentals, but press on

And the apostle Paul, in the next chapter to that wherein is the text,[1] counsels the Christian Hebrews, leaving the first principles of the doctrines of Christ, to go on to perfection. He would by no means have them always to

---

1. That is, of this message: Hebrews 5:12. Edwards apparently considered Paul to be the author of Hebrews.

rest only in those fundamental doctrines of repentance, and faith, and the resurrection from the dead, and the eternal judgment, in which they were instructed when baptized, at their first initiation in Christianity (see Heb. 6, etc.).

STUDY QUESTIONS

1. Review the previous chapter, together with this one. In your own words, summarize Edwards's case for growing in knowledge of divine truth. Do you find his arguments compelling? Why or why not?

2. Imagine yourself standing before God, giving an account of your stewardship of your calling as a "learner in the school of Christ." Take each of Edwards's arguments, one at a time, and explain yourself to the Lord. To what extent have you, to this point in your life, considered and heeded these arguments, and how is your response to them reflected in your study habits as a disciple of Christ?

3. Is there room for improvement in your life in this area of acquiring knowledge of divine truth? Among other things, improving this area will require better use of your time. What are some things that you might have to give up in order to make more time for growing in Christian knowledge? Do you consider that this sacrifice would be worthwhile?

4. Edwards says that learners must "take pains" to fulfill the calling appointed them by God. Learning is a difficult task (see Eccl. 1:13). As you think about beginning to devote yourself more diligently to this endeavor, what specific

kinds of "pains" do you anticipate having to address? What difficulties, struggles, and obstacles lie ahead for you? Keeping in mind the lesson of Edwards's first sermon, that all knowledge of God comes by his gracious Spirit, how might you prepare now, and in an ongoing way, to deal with these "pains"?

5. Let's begin with the things you are already doing to "strengthen the things that remain" (Rev. 3:2). In each of the following areas, how might you begin to take a more "businesslike" approach to growing in Christian knowledge?

a. Your daily devotions:

b. Your attention to preaching:

c. Your involvement in Bible studies:

d. Your personal reading and study:

❖ *Chapter 8* ❖

THE ADVANTAGES OF CHRISTIAN KNOWLEDGE

After a brief review of his argument thus far, Edwards launches into an explanation of the many advantages of taking up the business of devoting ourselves to gaining Christian knowledge. It is a better way to use our time and a noble endeavor. Growing in divine things is pleasant and can be very useful in the life of faith. We have great advantages and opportunities for growth available to us. And growing in divine things can help us to deal with adversity.

R E V I E W

Consider yourselves as scholars or disciples, put into the school of Christ; and therefore be diligent to make proficiency in Christian knowledge. Content not yourselves with this, that you have been taught your catechism in your childhood, and that you know as much of the principles of religion as is necessary to salvation; else you will be guilty of what the apostle warns against, viz., going no further than laying the foundation of repentance from good works, etc.

You are called to be Christians, and this is your profession. Endeavor, therefore, to acquire knowledge in things that pertain to your profession. Let not your teachers have cause to complain, that while they spend and are spent, to impart knowledge to you, you take little pains to learn. It is a great encouragement to an instructor to have such to teach as make a business of learning, bending their minds to it. This makes teaching a pleasure, when otherwise it would be a very heavy and burdensome task.

You all have by you a large measure of divine knowledge, in that you have the Bible in your hands; therefore be not contented in possessing but little of this treasure. God hath spoken much to you in the Scriptures; labor to understand as much of what he saith as you can. God hath made you all reasonable creatures; therefore let not the noble faculty of reason or understanding lie neglected. Content not yourselves with having so much knowledge as is thrown in your way, and [as you] receive in some sense unavoidably by the frequent inculcation of divine truth in the preaching of the Word, of which you are obliged to be hearers, or accidentally gain in conversation; but let it be very much your business to search for it, and that with the same diligence and labor with which men are wont to dig in mines of silver and gold.

Especially I would advise those who are young to employ themselves in this way. Men are never too old to learn; but the time of youth is especially the time for learning; it is peculiarly proper for gaining and storing up knowledge. Further, to stir up all, both old and young to this duty, let me entreat you to consider,

A Means of Profitable
Employment

1. If you apply yourselves diligently to this work, you will not want employment, when you are at leisure from your common secular business. In this way, you may find something in which you may profitably employ yourselves.

Rather than mere idling

You will find something else to do, besides going about from house to house, spending one hour after another in unprofitable conversation, or, at best, to no other purpose but to amuse yourselves, to fill up and wear away your time. And it is to be feared that very much of the time spent in evening visits is spent to a much worse purpose than that which I have now mentioned. Solomon tells us that "in the multitude of words there wanteth not sin" (Prov. 10:19). And is not this verified in those who find little else to do but to go to one another's houses, and spend the time in such talk as comes next, or such as anyone's present disposition happens to suggest?

Rather than always seeking diversion

Some diversion is doubtless lawful; but for Christians to spend so much of their time, so many long evenings, in no other conversation than that which tends to divert and amuse, if nothing worse, is a sinful way of spending time, and tends to poverty of soul at least, if not to outward poverty: "In all thy labor there is profit; but the talk of the lips tendeth only to *penury*" (Prov. 14:23). Besides, when persons for so much of their time have nothing else to do, but to sit, and talk, and chat, there is great danger of falling into foolish and sinful conversation, venting their corrupt dispositions in talking against others, expressing their jealousies and evil surmises concerning their neighbors; not considering what Christ hath said, "Of every idle word that men shall speak, shall they give account in the day of judgment" (Matt. 12:36).

Rather than dallying with temptation

If you would comply with what you have heard from this doctrine, you would find something else to employ your time besides contention, or talking about those public affairs which tend to contention. Young people might find something else to do, besides spending their time in vain company; something that would be much more profitable to themselves, as it would really turn to some good account; something, in doing which they would be both more out of the way of temptation, and be more in the way of duty, and of a divine blessing. And even aged people would have something to employ themselves in, after they are become incapable of bodily labor. Their time, as is now often the case, would not lie heavy upon their hands, as they would with both profit and pleasure be engaged in searching the Scriptures, and in comparing and meditating upon the various truths which they should find there.

A NOBLE INVESTMENT OF TIME

2. This would be a *noble* way of spending your time. The Holy Spirit gives the Bereans this epithet, because they dili-

gently employed themselves in this business: "These were more *noble* than those of Thessalonica, in that they received the word with all readiness of mind, and searched the Scriptures daily, whether those things were so" (Acts 17:11).

The employment of heaven

Similar to this is very much the employment of heaven. The inhabitants of that world spend much of their time in searching into the great things of divinity, and endeavoring to acquire knowledge in them, as we are told of the angels, "which things the angels desire to look into" (1 Peter 1:12).

Our employment for all eternity

This will be very agreeable to what you hope will be your business to all eternity, as you doubtless hope to join in the same employment with the angels of light. Solomon says, "It is the honor of kings to search out a matter" (Prov. 25:2); and certainly, above all others, to search out divine matters. Now, if this be the honor even of kings, is it not equally if not much more your honor?

A Pleasant Way of Improving Time

3. This is a pleasant way of improving time. Knowledge is pleasant and delightful to intelligent creatures, and above all, the knowledge of divine things; for in them are the most excellent truths, and the most beautiful and amiable objects held forth to view. However tedious the labor

necessarily attending this business may be, yet the knowledge once obtained will richly requite the pains taken to obtain it. "When wisdom entereth the heart, knowledge is pleasant to the soul" (Prov. 2:10).

THIS KNOWLEDGE USEFUL

4. This knowledge is exceedingly *useful* in Christian practice. Such as have knowledge in divinity have great means and advantages for spiritual and saving knowledge; for no means of grace have a saving effect, otherwise than by the knowledge they impart.

The better you will see God's glory

The more you have of a rational knowledge of divine things, the more opportunity will there be, when the Spirit shall be breathed into your heart, to see the excellency of these things, and to taste the sweetness of them. The heathens, who have no rational knowledge of the things of the gospel, have no opportunity to see the excellency of them; and therefore the more rational knowledge of these things you have, the more opportunity and advantage you have to see the divine excellency and glory in them.

The better you will do your duty

Again, the more knowledge you have of divine things, the better you will know your duty; your knowledge will be of great use to direct you as to your duty in particular cases. You will also be better furnished against the temptations of the devil. For the devil often takes advantage of persons' ignorance to ply them with temptations which otherwise would have no hold of them. By having much knowledge, you will be under greater advantages to conduct yourselves with prudence and discretion in your Christian course, and so to live much more to the honor of God and religion. Many who mean well and are full of a good spirit, yet for want of prudence, conduct themselves so as to wound religion. Many have zeal for God, which doth more hurt than good, because it is not according to knowledge (Rom. 10:2). The reason why many good men behave no better in many instances, is not so much that they want[1] grace, as that they want knowledge. Besides, an increase of knowledge would be a great help to profitable conversation. It would supply you with matter for conversation when you come together, or when you visit your neighbors: and so you would have less temptation to spend the time in such conversation as tends to your own and others' hurt.

ADVANTAGES TO GROWTH

5. Consider the advantages you are under to grow in the knowledge of divinity.

More of God's revelation
We are under far greater advantages to gain much of this knowledge now than God's people under the Old Tes-

1. Lack.

tament, both because the canon of Scripture is so much enlarged since that time, and also because evangelical truths are now so much more plainly revealed. So that common men are now in some respects under advantages to know more than the greatest prophets were then. Thus that saying of Christ is in a sense applicable to us, "Blessed are the eyes which see the things which ye see. For I tell you, that many prophets and kings have desired to see those things which ye see, and have not seen them; and to hear those things which ye hear, and have not heard them" (Luke 10:23–24).

Availability of printed material

We are in some respects under far greater advantages for gaining knowledge, now in these latter ages of the church, than Christians were formerly; especially by reason of the art of printing, of which God hath given us the benefit, whereby Bibles and other books of divinity are exceedingly multiplied, and persons may now be furnished with helps for the obtaining of Christian knowledge, at a much easier and cheaper rate than they formerly could.

STRENGTH TO DEFEND OURSELVES

We know not what opposition we may meet with in the religious principles which we hold. We know that there are many adversaries to the gospel and its truths. If therefore we embrace those truths, we must expect to be attacked by the said adversaries; and unless we be well informed concerning divine things, how shall we be able to defend ourselves? Besides, the apostle Peter enjoins it upon us always to be ready to give an answer to every man who asketh a reason of the faith that is in us. But this we cannot expect to do without considerable knowledge in divine things.

STUDY QUESTIONS

1. Edwards insists that those who believe in Jesus are called to the profession of being Christians. Every profession has standards and practices that bind its members. As we have seen in these first two sermons thus far, what standards and practices are those who profess Christ obliged to maintain?

2. Edwards believes that spending time reading and studying God's Word is much better than wasting time in frivolous diversions. If he had written this section today, as opposed to in the early eighteenth century, what kinds of diversions might he have singled out as time wasters? Do any of these tend to take up too much of your time? Why do we find these things so appealing, as compared with spending that time in, say, learning about the Lord?

3. Edwards maintains that growing in divine things is noble and pleasant. In what sense "noble"? Have you ever experienced intense, prolonged study of the Word of God as pleasant? In what way? Are there things that you find more pleasant than the study of God's Word (take a look at the way you use your time)? But are these things more noble?

4. It makes sense that the more we know of spiritual truth, the better able we will be to serve the Lord and resist the

enemy of our souls. Can you share an experience in which you saw this to be true in your life? Does it make sense to think that if you could learn more, you might expect to have more such experiences?

5. Do you think Edwards, if he had written the section on printing today, would want to expand that section? What kinds of things might he have included? Which of the many means and opportunities for growing in Christian knowledge are you currently making regular use of in your walk with the Lord?

❖ Chapter 9 ❖

GROWING IN CHRISTIAN KNOWLEDGE

As he concludes this sermon, Edwards offers seven wise and highly practical suggestions for beginning to make progress in acquiring knowledge of divine truth.

❖

[And now some] directions for the acquisition of Christian knowledge.

READ HOLY SCRIPTURE

1. Be assiduous in reading the Holy Scriptures. This is the fountain whence all knowledge in divinity must be derived. Therefore let not this treasure lie by you neglected. Every man of common understanding who can read, may, if he please, become well acquainted with the Scriptures. And what an excellent attainment would this be!

STUDY HOLY SCRIPTURE

2. Content not yourselves with only a cursory reading, without regarding the sense. This is an ill way of reading, to which, however, many accustom themselves all their days. When you read, observe what you read. Observe how things come in. Take notice of the drift of the discourse, and compare one Scripture with another. For the Scripture, by the harmony of its different parts, casts great light upon itself. We are expressly directed by Christ to *search* the Scriptures, which evidently intends something more than a mere cursory reading. And use means to find out the meaning of the Scripture. When you have it explained in the preaching of the Word, take notice of it; and if at any time a Scripture that you did not understand be cleared up to your satisfaction, mark it, lay it up, and if possible remember it.

STUDY BOOKS ON DIVINITY

3. Procure, and diligently use, other books which may help you to grow in this knowledge. There are many excellent books extant, which might greatly forward you in this knowledge, and afford you a very profitable and pleasant entertainment in your leisure hours. There is doubtless a great defect in many, that through a lothness to be at a little expense,[1] they furnish themselves with no more helps of this nature. They have a few books indeed, which now and

---

1. That is, a reluctance to spend money on books (imagine!).

then on Sabbath days they read; but they have had them so long, and read them so often, that they are weary of them, and it is now become a dull story, a mere task to read them.

IMPROVE CONVERSATION

4. Improve conversation with others to this end. How much might persons promote each other's knowledge in divine things, if they would improve conversation as they might; if men that are ignorant were not ashamed to show their ignorance, and were willing to learn of others; if those that have knowledge would communicate it, without pride and ostentation; and if all were more disposed to enter on such conversation as would be for their mutual edification and instruction.

LOOK FOR PRACTICAL APPLICATIONS

5. Seek not to grow in knowledge chiefly for the sake of applause, and to enable you to dispute with others; but seek it for the benefit of your souls, and in order to practice. If applause be your end, you will not be so likely to be led to the knowledge of the truth, but may justly, as often is the case of those who are proud of their knowledge, be led into error to your own perdition. This being your end, if you should obtain more rational knowledge, it would not be likely of any benefit to you, but would puff you up with pride: "Knowledge puffeth up" (I Cor. 8:1).

SEEK GOD'S DIRECTION
AND BLESSING

6. Seek to God, that he would direct you, and bless you, in this pursuit after knowledge. This is the apostle's direction: "If any man lack wisdom, let him ask it of God, who giveth to all liberally, and upbraideth not" (James 1:5). God is the fountain of all divine knowledge: "The Lord giveth wisdom: out of his mouth cometh knowledge and understanding" (Prov. 2:6). Labor to be sensible of your own blindness and ignorance, and your need of the help of God, lest you be led into error, instead of true knowledge: "If any man would be wise, let him become a fool, that he may be wise" (1 Cor. 3:18).

PRACTICE WHAT YOU LEARN

7. Practice according to what knowledge you have. This will be the way to know more. The psalmist warmly recommends this way of seeking knowledge in divine truth, from his own experience: "I understand more than the ancients, because I keep thy precepts" (Ps. 119:100). Christ also recommends the same: "If any man will do his will, he shall know of the doctrine, whether it be of God, or whether I speak of myself" (John 7:17).

STUDY QUESTIONS

1. Let's start thinking about a plan for growing in the knowledge of divine truth—growing in God's Spirit. Review

each of the seven sections in this chapter and assess your use of these suggestions by rating each on a scale of 1 to 10, with 10 being the highest and most favorable rating. Why did you select the number you did in each case?

a. Reading God's Word:
b. Studying God's Word:
c. Reading theological books:
d. Talking with others about spiritual truth:
e. Looking for practical applications:
f. Seeking God's direction and blessing:
g. Practicing what you learn:

2. In which of these recommendations do you need most improvement? What will it take for you to begin working on improving these areas? What can keep you from doing so? What will be the consequences of failing to do so? What might you expect if you could begin to improve these areas and start growing in God's Spirit?

3. How much of your weekly conversation with others is devoted to spiritual things? Edwards mentions several things that can keep us from becoming more involved in such conversations. What are they? What do you suppose it might take to help someone become "more disposed to enter on such conversation"? According to Edwards, what should be the goal of such conversations? How might we be able to tell when our contribution to any such conversations is contributing to realizing that goal?

4. Edwards reminds us, in section 6 of this chapter, that all learning comes from God—which was the point of his first

sermon in this series. This makes prayer, waiting on the Lord, reflection and meditation, and so forth very much important parts of the business of acquiring Christian knowledge. Can you think of some ways that you might begin to make prayer a more important part of your growth in God's Spirit? Is there someone you might link up with in a prayer relationship to encourage and pray with you? How might you expect to benefit from such a relationship?

5. Review the goals you set for this study at the end of chapter 1. Are you making any progress toward realizing them? In what ways? Do you need to revise your goals at all?

✱ *Part 3* ✱

THE CHRISTIAN PILGRIM

❀ Chapter 10 ❀

THE WAY OF THE TRAVELER

Having shown us how growing in God's Spirit takes place as we seek knowledge of divine things in the light of his Word and Spirit, Edwards now calls us to a lifetime of seeking the Lord in the way of holiness. He shows us that growing in God's Spirit has a particular focus and is a lifelong process that challenges us to become increasingly conformed to the vision of heaven and Christ.

❀

HEBREWS 11:13–14
And confessed that they were strangers and pilgrims on the earth. For they that say such things, declare plainly that they seek a country.

The apostle is here setting forth the excellencies of the grace of faith, by the glorious effects and happy issue of it in the saints of the Old Testament. He had spoken in the preceding part of the chapter particularly, of Abel, Enoch, Noah, Abraham and Sarah, Isaac and Jacob. Having enumerated those instances, he takes notice that "these all died in faith, not having received the promises, but having seen them afar off, were persuaded of them, and embraced them, and confessed that they were strangers," etc. In these words the apostle seems to have a more particular respect to Abraham and Sarah, and their kindred, who came with them from Haran, and from Ur of the Chaldees, as appears by the fifteenth verse, where the apostle says, "And truly if they had been mindful of that country from whence they came out, they might have had opportunity to have returned."

Two things may be observed here:

The confession of these great saints

1. What these saints confessed of themselves, viz., *that they were strangers and pilgrims on the earth.* Thus we have a particular account concerning Abraham, "I am a stranger and a sojourner with you" (Gen. 23:4). And it seems to have been the general sense of the patriarchs, by what Jacob says to Pharaoh: "And Jacob said to Pharaoh, The days of the years of my pilgrimage are an hundred and thirty years: few and evil have the days of the years of my life been, and have not attained to the days of the years of the life of my fathers in the days of their pilgrimage" (Gen. 47:9). "I am a stranger and a sojourner with thee, as all my fathers were" (Ps. 39:12).

The inference of the apostle

2. The inference that the apostle draws from hence, viz., *that they sought another country as their home.* "For they that say such things, declare plainly that they seek a country." In confessing that they were strangers, they plainly de-

clared that this is not their country; that this is not the place where they are at home. And in confessing themselves to be pilgrims, they declared plainly that this is not their settled abode; but that they have respect to some other country, which they seek, and to which they are traveling.

SEEK FIRST THE KINGDOM

Here I would observe,

Rest not in this world

1. That we ought not to rest in the world and its enjoyments, but should desire heaven. We should "seek first the kingdom of God" (Matt. 6:33). We ought above all things to desire a heavenly happiness; to be with God; and dwell with Jesus Christ. Though surrounded with outward enjoyments, and settled in families with desirable friends and relations; though we have companions whose society is delightful, and children in whom we see many promising qualifications; though we live by good neighbors, and are generally beloved where known; yet we ought not to take our rest in these things as our portion. We should be so far from resting in them, that we should desire to leave them all, in God's due time. We ought to possess, enjoy, and use them, with no other view but readily to quit them, whenever we are called to it, and to change them willingly and cheerfully for heaven.

Concentrate on the journey's end

A traveler is not wont to rest in what he meets with, however comfortable and pleasing, on the road. If he passes through pleasant places, flowery meadows, or shady groves, he does not take up his content in these things, but only takes a transient view of them as he goes along. He is not enticed by fine appearances to put off the thought of proceeding. No, but his journey's end is in his mind. If he meets with comfortable accommodations at an inn, he entertains no thoughts of settling there. He considers that these things are not his own, that he is but a stranger, and when he has refreshed himself, or tarried for a night, he is for going forward. And it is pleasant to him to think that so much of the way is gone.

So should we desire heaven more than the comforts and enjoyments of this life. The apostle mentions it as an encouraging, comfortable consideration to Christians, that they draw nearer their happiness. "Now is our salvation nearer than when we believed." Our hearts ought to be loose to these things, as that of a man on a journey; that we may as cheerfully part with them, whenever God calls. "But this I say, brethren, the time is short, it remaineth that both they that have wives be as though they had none; and they that weep, as though they wept not; and they that rejoice as though they rejoiced not; and they that buy as though they possessed not; and they that use this world, as not abusing it; for the fashion of this world passeth away" (1 Cor. 7:29–30). These things are only lent to us for a little while, to serve a present turn; but we should set our *hearts* on heaven, as our inheritance forever.

Holiness the Way of Heaven

2. We ought to seek heaven, by traveling in the way that leads thither. This is a way of holiness.

The way of holiness and no other

We should choose and desire to travel thither in this way and in no other; and part with all those carnal appetites which, as weights, will tend to hinder us. "Let us lay aside every weight, and the sin which doth so easily beset us, and let us run with patience the race set before us" (Heb. 12:1). However pleasant the gratification of any appetite may be, we must lay it aside, if it be a hindrance, or a stumbling block in the way to heaven.

The way of holiness the way of heaven

We should travel on in the way of obedience to all God's commands, even the difficult as well as the easy; denying all our sinful inclinations and interests. The way to heaven is ascending; we must be content to travel up hill, though it be hard and tiresome, and contrary to the natural bias of our flesh. We should follow Christ; the path he traveled, was the right way to heaven. We should take up our cross and follow him, in meekness and lowliness of heart, obedience and charity, diligence to do good, and patience under afflictions. The way to heaven is a heavenly life; an imitation of those who are in heaven, in their holy enjoyments, loving, adoring, serving, and praising God and the Lamb. Even if we *could* go to heaven with the gratification of our lusts, we should prefer a way of holiness and conformity to the spiritual self-denying rules of the gospel.

The way of holiness a laborious way

3. We should travel in this way in a laborious manner. Long journeys are attended with toil and fatigue; especially if through a wilderness. Persons in such a case expect no other than to suffer hardship and weariness. So we should travel in this way of holiness, improving our time and strength, to surmount the difficulties and obstacles that are in the way. The land we have to travel through is a wilderness; there are many mountains, rocks, and rough places that we must go over, and therefore there is necessity that we should lay out our strength.

The way of holiness our constant concern

4. Our whole lives ought to be spent in traveling this road. We ought to begin *early*. This should be the *first* concern, when persons become capable of acting. When they first set out in the *world* they should set out on *this* journey. And we ought to travel on with *assiduity*. It ought to be the work of every day. We should often think of our journey's end; and make it our daily work to travel on in the way that leads to it. He who is on a journey is often thinking of the destined place; and it is his daily care and business to get along; and to improve his time to get toward his journey's end. Thus should heaven be continually in our thoughts; and the immediate entrance or passage to it, viz., death,

should be present with us. We ought to *persevere* in this way as long as we live. "Let us run with patience the race that is set before us" (Heb. 12:1). Though the road be difficult and toilsome, we must hold out with patience, and be content to endure hardships. Though the journey be long, yet we must not stop short; but hold on till we arrive at the place we seek. Nor should we be discouraged with the length and difficulties of the way, as the children of Israel were, and be for turning back again. All our thought and design should be to press forward till we arrive.

GROW IN HOLINESS

5. We ought to be continually growing in holiness; and in that respect coming nearer and nearer to heaven.

Becoming more heavenly

We should be endeavoring to come nearer to heaven, in being more heavenly; becoming more and more like the inhabitants of heaven, in respect of holiness and conformity to God; the knowledge of God and Christ; in clear views of the glory of God, the beauty of Christ, and the excellency of divine things, as we come nearer to the beatific vision. We should labor to be continually growing in divine love—that this may be an increasing flame in our hearts, till they ascend wholly in this flame—in obedience and heavenly conversation; that we may do the will of God on earth as the angels do in heaven; in comfort and spiritual joy; in sensible communion with God, and Jesus Christ.

Our path should be "the shining light, that shines more to the perfect day" (Prov. 4:18). We ought to be hungering and thirsting after righteousness; after an increase in righteousness. "As newborn babes, desire the sincere milk of the word, that ye may grow thereby" (1 Peter 2:2). The perfection of heaven should be our mark. "This one thing I do, forgetting those things which are behind, and reaching forth unto those things that are before, I press toward the mark, for the prize of the high calling of God in Christ Jesus" (Phil. 3:13–14).

Subordinating all other concerns

6. All other concerns of this life ought to be entirely subordinate to this. When a man is on a journey, all the steps he takes are subordinated to the aim of getting to his journey's end. And if he carries money or provisions with him, it is to supply him in his journey. So we ought wholly to subordinate all our other business, and all our temporal enjoyments, to this affair of traveling to heaven. When anything we have becomes a clog and hindrance to us, we should quit it immediately. The use of our worldly enjoyments and possessions should be with such a view, and in such a manner, as to further us in our way heavenward. Thus we should eat, and drink, and clothe ourselves, and improve conversation and enjoyment of friends. And whatever business we are setting about, whatever design we are engaging in, we should inquire with ourselves, whether this business or undertaking will forward us in our way to heaven? And if not, we should quit our design.

STUDY QUESTIONS

1. Edwards stresses the importance of having a vision of heaven—a "beatific" vision—as our orienting and guiding vision in life. What do you suppose that involves? How do passages like Psalm 27:4 and Colossians 3:1–3 help you to think about this? How might a person go about nurturing such a vision and keeping it in focus throughout the day?

2. The way to heaven is the way of holiness, of growing in Christian knowledge through constant immersion in the divine and supernatural light of God. What are some of the indicators Edwards mentions that might suggest to a person that he or she is increasing in holiness?

3. What can keep us from pursuing holiness as the way to heaven? According to Edwards, should we expect this to be an easy or difficult journey? What would be examples in your experience of the kinds of "mountains," "rocks," and "rough places" (section 3) you might expect to encounter on your journey to heaven? How do you prepare yourself to go through or over these?

4. Look, in section 5, at each of the things Edwards mentions as landmarks in our journey to heaven. In which of these do you feel you need to make the most progress? Why?

   a. Holiness and conformity to God:
   b. Knowledge of God and Christ:
   c. Clear view of God's glory:
   d. Clear view of the beauty of Christ:

e. Clear view of the excellency of divine things:

f. Coming nearer to the beatific vision:

e. Increasing in love:

5. What should be the relationship between the things of this life—our work, families, possessions, and diversions—and our journey toward heaven? Can you give some examples of what this should look like in your own life? Do you think most Christians succeed fairly well at this part of their journey? Why or why not?

❧ Chapter 11 ❧

JOURNEY'S END

Edwards takes us aside to emphasize the importance of focusing on heaven and the vision of God and of seeing this life as merely a foretaste of and preparation for that ultimate destination to which our journey will take us.

❧

1. This world is not our abiding place. Our continuance here is very short. Man's days on the earth are as a shadow. It was never designed by God that this world should be our home. Neither did God give us these temporal accommodations for that end. If God has given us ample estates, and children or other pleasant friends, it is with no such design, that we should be furnished here, as for a settled abode; but with a design that we should use them for the present, and then leave them in a very little time.

OUR HOME IN THE FUTURE WORLD

Improve life for the journey

When we are called to any secular business, or charged with the care of a family, if we improve our lives to any other purpose than as a journey toward heaven, all our labor will be lost. If we spend our lives in the pursuit of temporal happiness; as riches or sensual pleasures; credit and esteem from men; delight in our children, and the prospect of seeing them well brought up, and well settled, etc.—all these things will be of little significance to us. Death will blow up all our hopes and will put an end to these enjoyments. "The places that have known us, will know us no more"; and "the eye that has seen us, shall see us no more." We must be taken away forever from all these things; and it is uncertain when: it may be soon after we are put into the possession of them. And then, where will be all our worldly employments and enjoyments, when we are laid in the silent grave? "So man lieth down and riseth not again, till the heavens be no more" (Job 14:12).

A lasting habitation

2. The future world was designed to be our settled and everlasting abode. There it was intended that we should be fixed; and there alone is a lasting habitation, and a lasting inheritance. The present state is short and transitory; but our state in the other world is everlasting. And as we are there at first, so we must be without change. Our state in the future world, therefore, being eternal, is of so much greater importance than our state here, that all our concerns in this world should be wholly subordinated to it.

GOD AND HEAVEN OUR HIGHEST GOOD

3. Heaven is that place alone where our highest end, and highest good, is to be obtained.

Made for God

God hath made us for himself. "Of him, and through him, and to him are all things." Therefore, then do we attain to our highest end, when we are brought to God: but that is by being brought to heaven; for that is God's throne, the place of his special presence. There is but a very imperfect union with God to be had in this world, a very imperfect knowledge of him in the midst of much darkness; a very imperfect conformity to God, mingled with abundance of estrangement. Here we can serve and glorify God but in a very imperfect manner; our service being mingled with sin, which dishonors God. But when we get to heaven (if ever that be), we shall be brought to a perfect union with God, and have more clear views of him. There we shall be fully conformed to God, without any remaining sin; for "we shall see him as he is." There we shall serve God perfectly; and glorify him in an exalted manner, even to the utmost powers and capacity of our nature. Then we shall perfectly give up ourselves to God; and our hearts will be pure and holy offerings, presented in a flame of divine love.

God our highest good

God is the highest good of the reasonable creature; and the enjoyment of him is the only happiness with which our souls can be satisfied. To go to heaven, fully to enjoy God, is *infinitely* better than the most pleasant accommodations here. Fathers and mothers, husbands, wives, or children, or the company of earthly friends, are but shadows; but the enjoyment of God is the substance. These are but scattered beams; but God is the sun. These are but streams; but God is the fountain. These are but drops; but God is the ocean. Therefore it becomes us to spend this life only as a journey toward heaven, as it becomes us to make the seeking of our highest end and proper good, the whole work of our lives; to which we should subordinate all other concerns of life. Why should we labor for, or set our hearts on, anything else, but that which is our proper end, and true happiness?

This World a Place of Preparation

4. Our present state, and all that belongs to it, is designed by him that made all things, to be wholly in order to another world. This world is made for a place of preparation for another. Man's mortal life was given him, that he might be prepared for his fixed state. And all that God has given us, is given to this purpose. The sun shines, and the rain falls upon us; and the earth yields her increase to this end. Civil, ecclesiastical, and family affairs, and all our personal concerns, are designed and ordered in subordination to a future world, by the maker and disposer of all things. To this therefore they ought to be subordinated by us.

Study Questions

1. This section is short but packed with important ideas. The first of these is the reiteration that heaven is our ultimate destination, and God is our highest good. Look at the fol-

lowing passages of Scripture. How does each of these help us to understand this idea better? What does each add to this idea:

a. Psalm 16:2, 11:
b. Psalm 73:27–28:
c. Ephesians 2:4–7:
d. Philippians 3:2–16:
e. Colossians 3:1–3:
f. Hebrews 12:1–2:

2. Peter says that we should be ready for people to ask us about the "hope" that we have (1 Peter 3:15). Suppose someone were to ask you just that. In the light of what we have seen thus far in this sermon, and the passages above, how would you explain the Christian's hope to someone else? To what extent does this hope fill your mind throughout the day?

3. The second idea to which Edwards returns several times in this section is that of the importance of subordinating all earthly and secular concerns to the purposes of the heavenly life. Reread this section. What kinds of concerns does Edwards include in this? Does he mean for us simply to forget about such things? Or not to become involved in them in any way? What does he intend? Take several of those areas and give some examples of what doing what Edwards calls for would look like.

4. If, as Edwards maintains, this world is a "preparation" for everlasting life in the world to come, how should people

outside the faith of Jesus expect to see in us that we are preparing for something different, something better? In what ways would our lives be different from theirs? What should be the role of growing in God's Spirit in this life of preparation?

5. How would you describe your vision of heaven at this time? Think about heaven, and being there forever with God. What do you see with your mind's eye? How strongly does this appeal to you? How often does this vision come into your mind during the day? Can you think of ways that a Christian might make this vision more constant and more compelling? Should he or she do so?

❈ Chapter 12 ❈

THE PERSPECTIVE OF
THE JOURNEY

In this section Edwards shows us how taking a pilgrim's perspective on life can help us to deal with the death of loved ones, keep us from lapsing into the way of sin, and encourage us to press on in tasting the good things of the Lord.

❈

THE PILGRIM'S PERSPECTIVE
ON DEATH

1. This doctrine may teach us moderation in our mourning for the loss of such dear friends, who, while they lived, improved their lives to right purposes. If they lived a holy life, then their lives were a journey toward heaven. And why should we be immoderate in mourning, when they are got to their journey's end?

Death a blessing to the Christian pilgrim

Death, though it appears to us with a frightful aspect, is to them a great blessing. Their end is happy, and better than their beginning. "The day of their death is better to them than the day of their birth" (Eccl. 7:1). While they lived, they desired heaven, and chose it above this world, or any of its enjoyments. For this they earnestly longed, and why should we grieve that they have obtained it? Now they have got to their Father's house. They find more comfort a thousand times, now they are got home, than they did in their journey. In this world they underwent much labor and toil; it was a wilderness they passed through. There were many difficulties in the way; mountains and rough places. It was laborious and fatiguing to travel the road; and they had many wearisome days and nights; but now they have got to their everlasting rest. "And I heard a voice from heaven, saying unto me, Write, blessed are the dead which die in the Lord, from henceforth: yea, saith the Spirit, that they may rest from their labors; and their works do follow them" (Rev. 14:13). They look back upon the difficulties, and sorrows, and dangers of life, rejoicing that they have surmounted them all.

The blessed state of the dead in Christ

We are ready to look upon death as their calamity, and to mourn that those who were so dear to us should be in the dark grave; that they are there transformed to corruption and worms; taken away from their dear children and enjoyments, etc., as though they were in awful circumstances. But this is owing to our infirmity; they are in a happy condition, inconceivably blessed. They do not mourn, but rejoice with exceeding joy: their mouths are filled with joyful songs, and they drink at rivers of pleasure. They find no mixture of grief that they have changed their mortal enjoyments, and the company of mortals, for heaven. Their life here, though in the best circumstances, was attended with much that was adverse and afflictive: but now there is an end to all adversity. "They shall hunger no more, nor thirst any more; neither shall the sun light on them, nor any heat. For the Lamb which is in the midst of the throne, shall feed them, and shall lead them unto living fountains of waters: and God shall wipe away all tears from their eyes" (Rev. 7:16–17).

Their blessed state our journey's destination

It is true, we shall see them no more in this world, yet we ought to consider that we are traveling toward the same place; and why should we break our hearts that they have got there before us! We are following after them, and hope, as soon as we get to our journey's end, to be with them again, in better circumstances. A degree of mourning for near relations when departed is not inconsistent with Christianity, but very agreeable to it; for as long as we are flesh and blood, we have animal propensities and affections. But we have just reason that our mourning should be mingled with joy. "But I would not have you to be ignorant, brethren, concerning them that are asleep, that ye sorrow not, even as others that have no hope" (1 Thess. 4:13), i.e., that they should not sorrow as the heathen, who had no knowledge of a future happiness. This appears by the following verse: "for if we believe that Jesus died and rose again, even so them also which sleep in Jesus, God will bring with him."

WARNING TO THOSE ON THE BROAD ROAD TO DESTRUCTION

2. If our lives ought to be only a journey toward heaven; how ill do they improve their lives that spend them in traveling toward hell!

The employment of the wicked

Some men spend their whole lives, from their infancy to their dying day, in going down the broad way to destruction. They not only draw nearer to hell as to time, but they every day grow more ripe for destruction; they are more assimilated to the inhabitants of the infernal world. While others press forward in the strait and narrow way to life, and laboriously travel up the hill toward Zion, against the inclinations and tendency of the flesh; these run with a swift career down to eternal death. This is the employment of every day, with all wicked men; and the whole day is spent in it. As soon as ever they awake in the morning, they set out anew in the way to hell, and spend every waking moment in it. They begin in early days. "The wicked are estranged from the womb, they go astray as soon as they are born, speaking lies" (Ps. 58:4). They hold on with perseverance. Many of them who live to be old are never weary in it; though they live to be a hundred years old, they will not cease traveling in this way to hell, till they arrive there.

And all the concerns of life are subordinated to this employment.

The wicked person a servant to sin

A wicked man is a servant of sin; his powers and faculties are employed in the service of sin, and in fitness for hell. And all his possessions are so used by him as to be subservient to the same purpose. Men spend their time in treasuring up wrath against the day of wrath. Thus do all unclean persons, who live in lascivious practices in secret; all malicious persons; all profane persons, that neglect the duties of religion. Thus do all unjust persons; and those who are fraudulent and oppressive in their dealings. Thus do all backbiters and revilers; all covetous persons, that set their hearts chiefly on the riches of this world. Thus do tavern haunters, and frequenters of evil company; and many other kinds that might be mentioned. Thus the bulk of mankind are hasting on the broad way to destruction; which is, as it were, filled up with the multitude that are going in it with one accord. And they are every day going into hell out of this broad way by thousands. Multitudes are continually flowing down into the great lake of fire and brimstone, as some mighty river constantly disembogues its water into the ocean.

Conversion but the Beginning of This Journey

3. Hence when persons are converted, they do but begin their work, and set out in the way they have to go. They

never till then do anything at that work in which their whole lives ought to be spent. Persons before conversion never take a step that way. Then does a man first set out on his journey, when he is brought home to Christ; and so far is he from having done his work, that his care and labor in his Christian work and business is then but begun, in which he must spend the remaining part of his life.

The converted must strive to increase

Those persons do ill, who when they are converted, and have obtained a hope of their being in a good condition, do not strive as earnestly as they did before, while they were under awakenings. They ought, henceforward, as long as they live, to be as earnest and laborious, as watchful and careful, as ever; yea, they should increase more and more. It is no just excuse, that now they have obtained conversion. Should not we be as diligent that we may serve and glorify God, as that we ourselves may be happy? And if we have obtained grace, yet we ought to strive as much that we may obtain the other degrees that are before, as we did to obtain that small degree that is behind. The apostle tells us that he forgot what was behind, and reached forth toward what was before (Phil. 3:13).

Striving for more of what we have seen

Yea, those who are converted have now a further reason to strive for grace; for they have seen something of its excellency. A man who has once tasted the blessings of Canaan has more reason to press toward it than he had before. And they who are converted should strive to "make their calling and election sure" (2 Peter 1:10). All those who are converted are not sure of it; and those who are sure, do not know that they shall be always so; and still seeking and serving God with the utmost diligence is the way to have assurance, and to have it maintained.

STUDY QUESTIONS

1. Edwards says we should mourn with those who mourn, but with moderation—a mourning mixed with joy. What reason does he give for this? How would you seek to comfort with joy one who had lost a loved one who knew the Lord?

2. What is the relationship between being able to mourn with joy and growing in God's Spirit? Can they expect to be prepared for the death of a redeemed loved one who have not pressed on to increase in the knowledge of divine truth? How can growing in God's Spirit help us to prepare for our death?

3. Edwards seems to believe that contemplation of heaven should be a principal preoccupation of our time in this life. How might a believer practice such contemplation? Do you think that most Christians think very much about heaven? Do you think their thoughts about heaven are as well informed as they might be? What does this challenge to be much in contemplation of heaven suggest about how our growth in Christian knowledge ought to proceed?

4. Many are not improving their lives for heaven but are still following the ways that characterize those on the broad road of destruction. How can believers help one another to leave that path and walk more consistently on the pilgrim's way? Take a look at Ephesians 4:17–24. How might a passage like this serve to help us assess our own daily walk?

5. Conversion is not the end of the life of faith, but the beginning. The rest of the life of one who has come to faith in Jesus Christ is a striving to improve that life. What is the role of growing in the Spirit in the life of faith? Why should we think of this calling as a "striving"? What obstacles or distractions can keep us from increasing in the knowledge of divine things? How can believers help one another to overcome those obstacles and distractions and continue to press on to what lies ahead?

❈ Chapter 13 ❈

LABOR FOR HEAVEN!

Edwards brings his sermon on the pilgrim's journey to an end by exhorting us to seek heaven above all else. If we will make heaven our end, and our lives a journey thereto, we will find strength to make life truly pleasant and meaningful, and to cope with death at life's end. His final "directions" tie this message firmly into the context of growing in God's Spirit which has guided us thus far.

Labor to obtain such a disposition of mind that you may choose heaven for your inheritance and home; and may earnestly long for it, and be willing to change this world, and all its enjoyments, for heaven. Labor to have your heart taken up so much about heaven, and heavenly enjoyments, as that you may rejoice when God calls you to leave your best earthly friends and comforts for heaven, there to enjoy God and Christ.

THE WAY THAT LEADS TO HEAVEN

Be persuaded to travel in the way that leads to heaven; viz., in holiness, self-denial, mortification, obedience to all the commands of God, following Christ's example; in a way of a heavenly life, or imitation of the saints and angels in heaven. Let it be your daily work, from morning till night, and hold out in it to the end; let nothing stop or discourage you, or turn you aside from this road. And let all other concerns be subordinate to this. Consider the reasons that have been mentioned why you should thus spend your life; that this world is not your abiding place, that the future world is to be your everlasting abode; and that the enjoyments of this world are given entirely in order to another. And consider further for motive,

The worthiness of heaven

1. How worthy is heaven that your life should be wholly spent as a journey toward it. To what better purpose can you spend your life, whether you respect your duty or your interest? What better end can you propose to your journey, than to obtain heaven? You are placed in this world, with a choice given you, that you may travel which way you please; and one way leads to heaven. Now, can you direct your course better than this way? All men have some aim or other in living. Some mainly seek worldly things; they spend their days in such pursuits. But is not heaven, where is fullness of joy forever, much more worthy to be sought by you? How can you better employ your strength, use your means, and spend your days, than in traveling the road that leads to the everlasting enjoyment of God; to his glorious presence; to the new Jerusalem; to the heavenly Mount Zion; where all your desires will be filled, and no

danger of ever losing your happiness? No man is at home in this world, whether he choose heaven or not; here he is but a transient person. Where can you choose your home better than in heaven?

The way to make death comfortable

2. This is the way to have death comfortable to us. To spend our lives so as to be only a journeying toward heaven, is the way to be free from bondage, and to have the prospect and forethought of death comfortable. Does the traveler think of his journey's end with fear and terror? Is it terrible to him to think that he has almost got to his journey's end? Were the children of Israel sorry, after forty years' travel in the wilderness, when they had almost got to Canaan? This is the way to be able to part with the world without grief. Does it grieve the traveler when he has got home, to quit his staff and load of provisions that he had to sustain him by the way?

No more pleasant way of life

3. No more of your life will be pleasant to think of when you come to die, than has been spent after this manner. If you have spent none of your life this way, your whole life will be terrible to you to think of, unless you die under some great delusion. You will see, then, that all of your life that has been spent otherwise is lost. You will see then the vanity of all other aims that you may have proposed to yourself. The thought of what you here possessed and enjoyed will not be pleasant to you, unless you can think also that you have subordinated them to this purpose.

Heaven free for those desiring it

4. Consider that those who are willing thus to spend their lives as a journey toward heaven may have heaven. Heaven, however high and glorious, is attainable for such poor worthless creatures as we are. We may attain that glorious region which is the habitation of angels; yea, the dwelling place of the Son of God; and where is the glorious presence of the great Jehovah. And we may have it freely; without money and without price: if we are but willing to travel the road that leads to it, and bend our course that way as long as we live, we may and shall have heaven for our eternal resting place.

Our lives a journey—either to heaven, or to hell

5. Let it be considered that if our lives be not a journey toward heaven, they will be a journey to hell. All mankind, after they have been here a short while, go to either of the two great receptacles of all that depart out of this world: the one is *heaven*; whither a small number, in comparison, travel; and the other is *hell,* whither the bulk of mankind throng. And one or the other of these must be the issue of our course in this world.

CONCLUDING DIRECTIONS

I shall conclude by giving a few *directions*.

See the vanity of this world

1. Labor to get a sense of the vanity of this world; on account of the little satisfaction that is to be enjoyed here;

its short continuance, and unserviceableness when we most stand in need of help, viz., on the death bed. All men that live any considerable time in the world might see enough to convince them of its vanity, if they would but consider. Be persuaded therefore to exercise consideration, when you see and hear, from time to time, of the death of others. Labor to turn your thoughts this way. See the vanity of the world in such a glass.

Be much acquainted with heaven

2. Labor to be much acquainted with heaven. If you are not acquainted with it, you will not be likely to spend your life as a journey thither. You will not be sensible of its worth, nor will you long for it. Unless you are much conversant in your mind with a better good, it will be exceeding difficult to you to have your hearts loose from these things, and to use them only in subordination to something else, and be ready to part with them for the sake of that better good. Labor therefore to obtain a realizing sense of a heavenly world, to get a firm belief of its reality, and to be very much conversant with it in your thoughts.

Seek heaven through Jesus Christ

3. Seek heaven only by Jesus Christ. Christ tells us that he is the way, and the truth, and the life (John 14:6). He tells us that he is the door of the sheep. "I am the door, by me if any man enter in he shall be saved; and go in and out and find pasture" (John 10:9). If we therefore would improve our lives as a journey toward heaven, we must seek it

by him, and not by our own righteousness; as expecting to obtain it only for his sake, looking to him, having our dependence on him, who has procured it for us by his merit. And expect strength to walk in holiness, the way that leads to heaven, only from him.

Help one another in this journey

Let Christians help one another in going this journey. There are many ways whereby Christians might greatly forward one another in their way to heaven, as by religious conference, etc. Therefore let them be exhorted to go this journey as it were in company, conversing together, and assisting one another. Company is very desirable in a journey, but in none so much as this. Let them go united, and not fall out by the way, which would be to hinder one another; but use all means they can to help each other up the hill. This would insure a more successful traveling, and a more joyful meeting at their Father's house in glory.

STUDY QUESTIONS

1. Edwards indicates that seeking heaven involves pursuing holiness in the Lord. This is the way to ensure that we are on the path that leads to heaven. Look at 2 Corinthians 6:12—7:1. What seems to be the thrust of Paul's argument in these verses? In what ways does it parallel Edwards's thoughts in the first part of this chapter?

2. The writer of Hebrews says that people spend all their lives in fear of death (Heb. 2:15). In what ways have you

seen this to be true? How does laboring to travel the road that leads to heaven help us to overcome this fear?

3. Edwards calls us to "be much acquainted with heaven." What passages in God's Word come to mind when you think about heaven? What do you learn from these passages about what heaven will be like? How might you be able to use passages such as these to "turn your thoughts" to heaven during the course of the day?

4. As in his sermon on Christian knowledge, Edwards believes Christians can help one another in traveling the road to heaven by spending time together, talking about heaven, and encouraging one another in the way. Do you think study and discussion of heaven should be more a subject of our Christian education than is currently the case? Why or why not? How might Christians expect to benefit if instruction about heaven, and the desirability of the way thereto, were more a part of their Christian education from the earliest years on?

5. Review the goals you set for this study of Edwards on growing in God's Spirit. Did you reach any of your goals? Which? What new ideas for study or growth have these three sermons prompted in you? In what ways would you like to discover more of what it means to grow in God's Spirit?

INDEX OF SCRIPTURE